Cooking with Microgreens

cooking with
MICROGREENS

THE GROW-YOUR-OWN
Superfood

The Countryman Press
Woodstock, VT
www.countrymanpress.com

SAL GILBERTIE
LARRY SHEEHAN

Published by The Countryman Press, P.O. Box 748, Woodstock, VT 05091

Distributed by W. W. Norton & Company, Inc., 500 Fifth Avenue, New York, NY 10110

Printed in the United States of America

Cooking with Microgreens
978-1-58157-266-7

10 9 8 7 6 5 4 3 2 1

Henry Beary

Henry Beary

Contents

Peter Novajosky

PART 1

Growing Microgreens

Henry Beary

Introduction

Growing microgreens at home is the closest thing to a personal salad bar as you can get. With very little space—a kitchen windowsill, a tabletop in a spare room, or any other grow-your-own setup you may improvise—and just average or better light conditions, you can produce crop after crop of clean and scrumptious greens to keep the home cook well supplied and happy.

Because, as it turns out, really good taste comes in small packages. First-time consumers of microgreens are often taken aback by the potent flavors they encounter. The unexpected pleasure of savoring real corn flavor in the green shoots we grow from corn seed is one of my favorite rewards in raising microgreens. Tiny radish greens taste of radish with oomph, pretty red-stemmed beet greens have the earthiness of beets, and garden cress packs the peppery zest of the mustard and watercress to which it is related. The various micro varieties of chard are even sweeter and more colorful than beets, pea shoots are as tasty as peas themselves, purple cabbage surprises with its sweet but mild cabbage flavor, and celery, though it is harder to grow than many microgreens, rewards with the essence of mature celery.

Not only do these immature leaves of herbs, salad greens, edible flowers (nasturtiums and pansies, for example), and leafy vegetables provide a host of different ways to add crunch, color, and flavor to salads, sandwiches, soups, and other dishes. Microgreens also deliver nutrition to you and your family with minimal effort and cost. Recent studies have shown that these miniature versions of grown-up greens are packed with many times the vitamins and minerals found in mature versions of the same crop.

This is due to the fact that in making the transition from seed to leaf, the young plant is powered by its exceptional nutrient content. It is not unlike the nutrient power packed in the nucleus of an egg. One medical doctor compares eating microgreens to taking vitamin supplements—but with more tangible health benefits.

Researchers at the University of Maryland have determined that red cabbage microgreens contain a mind-boggling forty times more vitamin E and six times more vitamin C than mature red cabbage. Cilantro microgreens have three times more beta carotene, a powerful antioxidant, than fully developed cilantro. Some "micros" contain even more beta carotene than carrots, the beta carotene champ. Other studies point to broccoli microgreens and some of broccoli's Asian relatives, such as pac choi and daikon radish, as so rich in dietary antioxidants, they may well deter the incidence or severity of diabetes, cardiovascular disease, and some cancers.

Without getting too technical, it can be noted that antioxidants are believed to protect healthy cells from the damage caused by unstable molecules known as free radicals. Besides beta carotene, lycopene and vitamins A, C, and E have all been identified as antioxidants. All out of proportion to their age and size, microgreens contain such helpful substances in large amounts. One recent study published by the American Society for Horticultural Science reveals that lettuce seedlings, harvested seven days after germination, had higher antioxidant capacity than mature plants.

Let's face it, you're probably not going to consume enough microgreens in the course of your daily diet to go from 110-pound weakling to Incredible Hulk, bursting with strength and energy. But you will certainly reap the nutritional rewards of what has been called the new superfood. Rarely has such good medicine tasted so great.

And blending several varieties of microgreens creates taste sensations that are greater than the sum of their parts. All of the most popular blends we put together at Gilbertie's Herb Gardens & Petite Edibles for restaurant chefs and home cooks can be created in your own microgreens garden. Our Asian blend emits the flavors and aromas of the Far East in the form of tatsoi, shungkiku, and red pac choi. Renee's French blend offers a classic combination of beets, chervil, garlic, and purple basil that's like a culinary journey through Provence. Lemon basil, sorrel, and red amaranth add eye-popping color and zesty flavor to our Citrus blend.

A friend of mine recently went to New York City to see a play. Before the performance, she had dinner at Café Un Deux Trois: roasted salmon with mashed potatoes garnished with microgreens. The next day she met a friend for lunch at the Museum of Modern Art. In the museum café (menu by Danny Meyer of Union Square Café fame), the three small appetizers she ordered came with a generous salad of microgreens. For dinner that night at the Knickerbocker, she ordered liver (because her husband won't let her cook it at home). It came with roasted sweet potatoes on a bed of microgreens.

Afterward, she told me she was somewhat surprised that no one had served up microgreens during the play she attended!

Peter Novajosky

Well, you get the idea. Mixing and matching microgreens does wonders for salads and for entrées of all kinds. One of my favorite fish recipes, haddock baked with olive oil, butter, and bread crumbs and topped with parsley and dill, gets a professional finishing touch when served on a generous amount of lemon-flavored greens. (Extra-virgin olive oil, by the way, is believed to improve the body's absorption of nutrients from microgreens.) Brussels sprouts, baked or broiled, are enlivened when served atop a spicy blend of mustards, lettuces, and nasturtium. Breakfast becomes a robust brunch with the last-minute addition of an earthy mesclun blend to an omelet or a simple dish of scrambled eggs.

Taste, more than the obvious health benefits, is what has triggered the microgreens revolution in America. No one knows for sure who first came up with the idea of adding these greens to recipes, but the inspiration surely stemmed from the organic farming and gardening movement that has gained so much impetus and popularity in recent years.

Microgreens began to appear on the scene in Southern California in the mid-1990s. Johnny's Selected Seeds first listed microgreens in its catalog in 2001. Some say renowned Chicago restaurateur Charlie Trotter, who died at a young age a few scant years ago, was one of the first chefs to encourage farmers to grow microgreens, as he searched for a viable alternative to mesclun, the fresh salad mix of arugula, chervil, and various lettuces that had become commonplace on menus. For example, in the late 1980s he encouraged Lee Jones of the Chef's Garden farm in Huron, Ohio, to grow micro lettuces and baby beets and cabbage. "Charlie was also the first to ask us to grow purple Brussels sprouts!" Lee recalls.

In any case, microgreens were developed by organic farmers as a direct result of the demand of chefs catering to their urbane, sophisticated diners. It was a nationally celebrated chef, in fact, Gerard Clinton of Aspetuck Valley Country Club here in Easton, Connecticut, who several years ago first approached me with the idea of growing herbs and other greens in trays for cutting. Gilbertie's Herb Gardens & Petite Edibles had been in the business of growing hundreds of varieties of potted herb plants on our farm in Easton, which includes four acres of greenhouse space, primarily for sale to retail garden centers up and down the Eastern Seaboard. At first I was skeptical, but went ahead and planted up a full greenhouse bench, holding 30 sowing trays each measuring 10" x 20", of a dozen or so varieties of cilantro, dill, mustard greens, pac choi, and other greens. Weeks later, Gerard was champing at the bit to take the freshly harvested microgreens back to his kitchen, and he quickly spread the word to other chefs in the area about the unexpected bounty. Thanks to Lloyd Allen, the owner of Double L Market in Westport, Connecticut, I was also able to test-market microgreens in a retail food store, where customers enthusiastically snatched up the produce.

Today we grow more than 50 varieties of microgreens for over 60 restaurants in the New York metropolitan area. We also supply numerous country clubs, organic food stores, and farmer's markets with our product. Dozens and dozens of farmers in other parts of the country have also tailored their crop production to meet local demand for quality organic greens, known in the trade as "artisanal produce." The standards for commercial microgreen farming even at a local level are so high that large agribusiness entities do not appear to be interested in this particular market. Labor is too intensive, organic methods are too complex, and perishability is too much of a factor for large-scale growers to invest in the field, at least for now. Hooray for the little guy!

Yet for an individual gardener to grow microgreens in a home setting is not much of a challenge so long as you follow sound organic-gardening practices and stay on top of your precious plantings, with daily inspections. "The eye of the farmer makes the pig fat."

What exactly are microgreens? They are young, tender, edible crops that are

Peter Novajosky

harvested as shoots or seedlings. These tiny plants are grown to the first true leaf, which comes after the appearance of two kidney-shaped seed leaves, or cotyledons. Cotyledons spring from the seed embryo, while true leaves develop from the plant stem. Some varieties reach the true leaf stage so quickly that they can be cut for eating after the first week or two, when they will have reached about 1½ to 2 inches in height. True microgreens, these include such popular salad staples as lettuce, cress, kale, radishes, and mustard greens. Other greens are best harvested when they reach a height of 2 to 3 inches. Often labeled "petite edibles," these varieties include beets, broccoli, red cabbage, spinach, and many lettuce varieties. Finally, so-called baby greens are usually left to develop clustered leaves and a height of 3 to 5 inches. Arugula, spinach, dill, fennel, parsley, and kohlrabi are among the greens that benefit from delayed harvest times by filling out more completely.

To a certain extent these differences among microgreen varieties are subject to nuances of language. For the sake of clarity, when we use the term "microgreens," we are referring generally to seedlings and shoots at all stages of growth. Micro-greens may cost more, but the consumer obtains more flavor and nutrition from them, so they are well worth the extra expense. Of course, if you grow your own, price is not a factor. Farmers base their wholesale prices on weight, so it is in their financial interest to grow conventional greens to their maximum volume. In any event, the home gardener will be primarily concerned with quality, not quantity. In general, every species of green, whether it is classified as microgreen, petite edible, or baby green, should be harvested when it is at its peak in flavor and texture. It doesn't take more than two or three production cycles for home gardeners to deter-mine the very best strategies for harvesting specific varieties at their optimal stages of growth.

Microgreens should not be confused with sprouts, which are germinated seeds lacking true leaves. Sprouts were the signature garnish of the rebellious, back-to-the-earth 1970s generation, and they are still a favorite food group for many, even though care must be taken to prevent sprouts, nurtured in dark, moist conditions, from being contaminated with viral or bacterial agents. There have been E. coli and salmonella outbreaks attributed to sprouts, and even a small number of deaths from eating sprouts have been reported in Europe as recently as 2011.

Microgreens, grown in an organic soil mix under conditions of good air circulation and light, are much less susceptible to worrisome health issues.

In our greenhouses, we sow microgreens in rows in 10" x 20" plastic trays, or flats, filled to 2 to 3 inches with our own organic soil blend. (It takes 6 quarts of soil to fill a single tray.) The bottoms of the trays have drainage holes for letting water seep out to prevent soggy soil. Using a ridged wooden press that fits snugly within the 10" x 20" framework, we create shallow, straight rows to receive the seed—usually seven rows per flat for maximum productivity, depending on the variety. After sowing, we irrigate by hand with a gentle water spray. We continue spraying to keep the seedbed moist, but not soaking wet, until germination occurs.

Germination rates vary greatly depending on the plant variety—from three days to three weeks. That's why, when sowing more than one variety in a single tray, it's important to select crops that will germinate and grow out at the same rate.

Scatter sowing, or broadcasting, seed across the soil bed, instead of in straight rows, works with some seed varieties better than others. Micros like basil, chervil, and cilantro do better planted in rows. Beets, peas, and wheatgrass take well to scatter sowing. For the sake of productivity, it's important that all seed be evenly distributed.

After germination, we irrigate the greens not from above but at the base of the plants. This keeps soil from splashing up on the seedlings. Bottom watering will also discourage rot, mold, and fungus. In a greenhouse operation, we have the luxury of controlling the heat and light that our plantings are exposed to, so there are few if any developmental problems, but it is always important to watch for fungus. Overly wet conditions may invite insect pests such as aphids, whitefly, thrips, and leafhoppers. (Some seed catalogs offer a handy rogue's gallery of photos showing exactly what these unwelcome guests look like.) Birds can also be a problem, believe it or not, even in the confines of greenhouses. We keep marauding sparrows away from our fresh sowings of basil and sorrel, which for some reason are high on the list of avian treats, by diverting them to bird feeders filled with sunflower seed just outside our greenhouse range.

We harvest microgreens with sharp, long-bladed, hygienically sterile scissors. There are a variety of harvest and field knife models that will also do the job. From the time of sowing it will take from two to four weeks for greens to reach harvest stage. A few crops are slower to mature and so demand more time in the gestation stages. Winter sowings generally take a week or two longer to mature than warm-weather sowings. After the harvest, we transfer spent soil to our compost pile and wash the used trays with a mild bleach-and-water solution. Then we refill trays with a fresh soil mix, and begin the sowing-watering-harvesting cycle all over again. Timely sowing of new flats of greens insures a continuous supply of favorite greens—a river of nutrition that never runs dry.

Exact harvest amounts will vary according to how thickly greens are sown and at what stage they are cut. A typical yield from a single tray of arugula or mustard is approximately a third of a pound. More prolific growers like peas and radishes may produce as much as half a pound. Those amounts don't sound astronomical, but they represent a lot of crunchy, tasty salads for your family's weekly menu.

At Gilbertie's, we pack fresh greens for retail customers in 2- to 5-ounce clear plastic "clamshell" containers (so called for the way they open and close). We deliver greens to restaurants packed loosely in ½-pound or 1-pound plastic bags, always within 24 hours (or less) of harvest. For home use, most growers harvest their greens at the time and in the amount they are needed in salads or other recipes. A surplus of greens can also be stored in the refrigerator in plastic bags or other containers for later use in food preparation. Generally, greens will retain their fresh flavor and texture for up to 10 to 14 days when refrigerated. Most home chefs will make use of their greens as soon after harvest as practical.

What microgreens should you grow? It all depends on your taste preferences, of course, and how you want to use them in recipes. In this book, you will find plant profiles of some 50 microgreens, all worth your consideration for growing at home. For now, let's group some of the most desirable micros by their degree of difficulty in terms of cultivation.

The microgreens *most difficult to grow,* because of their slowness to germinate and to harvest, include the following:

- Amaranth
- Basil (all varieties)
- Chives
- Lemongrass
- Mâche
- Red-Veined Sorrel

Microgreens that are *less difficult to grow,* but still dependent on more growing time and attention, include:

- Beets
- Broccoli
- Cabbage
- Chervil
- Cilantro
- Dill
- Fennel
- Kohlrabi
- Lettuce (all varieties)
- Parsley
- Spinach
- Sorrel

And here are the microgreens *easiest to grow,* from which I suggest you make your choices for your first growing experiments:

- Arugula
- Cress
- Corn
- Kale

Microgreens and Kids: The Perfect Match

If you have children, cultivating microgreens in your own home provides a great way to introduce them to the joys of gardening. Micro peas and radishes, to name just two varieties you might want to try with youngsters, germinate and grow so quickly that there isn't time for a child to grow bored with the project. The magical emergence of seedlings in just a few days teaches them all about seed power, soil fertility, and the indispensable role of water and light in making things grow. It's a neat project for those winter weekends when there isn't anything to do outside, but it can succeed at any time of year.

By growing their own microgreens, children learn, without the tedium often associated with a lecture or lesson, that vegetables come from the earth, not from cans and boxes, and that the human hand of the farmer is as indispensable to the process as a pianist's fingers are to the music that comes from a piano. At the same time, children learn to appreciate the great taste and value of homegrown greens. When kids start reaching for lettuce to add to their hamburgers and BLTs, or pea shoots to put atop their grilled cheese sandwiches, you know you've done your job as a parent or teacher.

Speaking of education, at the invitation of a nonprofit group called Green Village Initiative, I introduced microgreens gardening as a classroom project to dozens of teachers in the Bridgeport, Connecticut, elementary school system. I gave each teacher a set of four berry boxes with plastic inlays filled with our organic soil mix, and four packets of fast-germinating seed varieties—peas, radishes, mesclun, and corn. It was the dead of winter at the time and the teachers were eager to get their kids started. They already had their classroom windows picked out for the growing stations, and they borrowed trays from the school cafeterias to deploy the berry boxes—schoolteachers are just as resourceful as farmers!—ready for sowing and watering by their pupils.

I should mention that GVI, based in Westport, Connecticut (www. gogvi. org), has built exemplary community gardens and hands-on "edible gardens" for children in numerous schools statewide. I'm so proud to be a volunteer in their campaign for growing healthy local food, empowering young people to grow and enjoy good food, and having fun along the way.

So please don't hesitate to use your own microgreens garden as a classroom for kids. The experience will be rewarding for everyone involved.

- Mesclun
- Mizuna
- Pac Choi
- Peas
- Mustards

- Nasturtiums
- Sunflowers
- Shungiku
- Yukina savoy

Now that we've whetted your appetite for microgreens, let's get to work actually growing them.

Growing Microgreens at Home

Finding a good location for growing microgreens in your house or apartment may be easier than you think. Starting tomato seedlings or other fruit-producing crops indoors requires direct sunlight over a long period of time. Grow lights are often employed for long-term indoor gardening. But microgreens germinate and grow fast even in indirect light. Of course, the more sun the better, but with microgreens, more so than with standard-size crops, you can get away with less sun. The less direct sunlight, the more the tiny plants will stretch as they reach for light. But when plants are ready to harvest in two or three weeks' time, they won't really have had time to get very leggy.

There are many locations that can be adapted for use as a microgreens garden. An old farm table under a bank of windows in the kitchen or a spare room may give you more than enough space to grow all the microgreens you want. Windowsills deep enough to accommodate plastic seedling trays could also work. Simple plywood extensions built off narrow windowsills can be utilized to create the amount of working surface area you need. Many gardeners have learned to winter over tender flowering plants, such as geraniums or begonias, in corners of a dwelling that are reasonably well lighted and warm enough—55 to 60 degrees Fahrenheit—to nurture plant life. Porches, balconies, and terraces often can be adapted for tending

Peter Novajosky

microgreens, at least when winter temperatures are not a factor. Some microgreen varieties will do well when sown in an outside plot, but the home gardener has much better control of the growing conditions when the plants are in containers in protected indoor areas.

Having settled on a good location for our project, let's now review the materials and techniques we need to be familiar with.

CONTAINERS

Microgreens will grow in just about any receptacle, but for practical purposes I suggest using easily obtainable standard-measure containers. The 10" x 20" plastic seedling trays in universal use at garden centers and greenhouses can serve as your basic vessel for holding and growing microgreens. (In the trade, these trays are called "1020s.") Seedling trays feature holes or slots in the bottom, essential for good drainage. A relatively small amount of potting soil—6 quarts—will fill the tray to the most desirable depth of about 2½ inches. The tray can then be sowed in linear rows with seed, or scatter-sowed if you prefer.

Moisture will be released through the perforations in the seedling tray, after periodic waterings of your seed and plants, so take care to protect any wood surfaces on which trays are placed. The simplest solution is to cradle the tray in a larger container lined with a single layer of loose pebbles or

Peter Novajosky

gravel. There are hard plastic trays measuring 11" x 22", available through garden centers and some garden catalogs, that make an ideal holding vessel for seedling trays. Because they have no irrigation holes, these trays will contain overflow moisture, keeping water off tables, windowsills, or garden carts, and, when properly maintained, prevent fungus from developing in and around the soil bed.

How much space should you allocate for your microgreens garden? A single person might be happy with two or three seedling trays if plantings are scheduled to enable continuous harvests. A salad-loving family of four might require four to six seedling trays to meet their needs.

Containers other than the plastic 1020 seedling trays described here are also fine for microgreens, provided the fundamentals of good growing are observed.

Peter Novajosky

Sturdy, inexpensive food-storage containers can be converted into seedling trays by drilling ¼-inch drainage holes in the bottom. Food-storage containers come in many different sizes, and they are often available at bargain prices at tag sales, garage sales, and flea markets. Look for relatively shallow ones that you can fill with 2 to 3 inches of soil. Lids can be used as trays to contain the water that drains through the holes.

Terra cotta pots, shallow wood boxes, plastic clamshell produce containers, and just about any other vessel that will hold soil and tolerate water can also be used to raise your favorite micros. Repurposed containers will give you the same results as the seedling trays used by growers, just as long as the right techniques, care, and attention are brought to the growing process.

Peter Novajosky

To make seedling trays amenable to growing a variety of microgreens, there are two approaches to consider. One is to make multiple sowings in a single seedling tray. For example, sow three rows of one micro and four rows of another in the same tray. Or devote two rows each to a different crop, and sow the seventh row with a micro you haven't tried before.

The other way to diversify crop selection is to choose from a wide range of smaller, inexpensive planting containers that can be fitted together into the same seedling tray. Eight 5½-inch-square pressed cardboard baskets (the familiar kind seen overflowing with blueberries and raspberries at farm stands in the summer) fit snugly in a single 10" x 20" seedling tray. The useful life of berry boxes can be extended if hard plastic boxes are placed inside them as waterproof liners. Baskets known as fiber packs with similar dimensions but made from recycled cardboard are also available through garden supply stores and catalogs. Fill each planting pod with soil, then scatter sow with your choice of microgreen seeds.

SOIL

The organic medium we mix ourselves for all our plantings consists of 30 percent topsoil, 30 percent compost, 30 percent peat moss, and 10 percent perlite. Given the small amount of planting medium required for growing microgreens at home, it's generally not worth the time and effort to mix your own. A 1020 seedling tray takes about three quarts of planting medium to fill to an arable height, so a small bag or two of commercial sterilized potting soil, usually packed 16 to 24 quarts to the bag, is probably all you will need to get started. Topsoil is cheaper by the bag, but it is too heavy for sowing microgreens. Also, avoid using soil transferred from an existing outdoor garden, as it may contain undesirable elements. Shop around to find a mix that is clearly marked organic and that contains some organic fertilizer such as kelp or shrimp meal. Because this product is packed in relatively heavy bags, weighing 25 pounds or more, it is usually too costly to ship long distances. That's why different regions of the country are likely to be supplied with soil mixes from various origins. Organic mixes produced by Coast of Maine are readily available at many nurseries and garden centers in the Northeast, for example. They may cost a dollar or two more per bag but the quality of the mix, which usually contains extra nutrients from its seafood additives, is well worth the price. In other regions of the country, there are similar reliable sources of organic soil mix for your microgreens garden.

Bear in mind that if soil temperature is under 55 degrees Fahrenheit, seed germination of the micro plants will take much longer. So, depending on where it has been stored, if you buy potting soil in the early spring months, it may be necessary to let it warm up in an indoor location for a couple of days before use.

SEED

Today there are plenty of reliable suppliers of organic seed to choose from. Avoid all seed treated with chemical fungicides when ordering. It is more economical to buy seed from catalog purveyors than in seed packets off the rack in stores. In some of these miserly seed-rack packets, there may not be enough seed to sow more than one of the seven seed rows in your seedling tray.

Some purveyors package their seed by actual seed count. Chef's Garden in Ohio, for example, labels a "large" packet of corn as containing 600 to 700 seeds. A large packet of their arugula contains 1,000 to 1,200 arugula seeds.

The majority of seed companies, however, package and sell their seed by weight in ounces and pounds, offering starter amounts by packet but listing better-priced seed in larger quantities, typically by the 1 ounce, ¼ pound, 1 pound, and up to 5 pounds, a fairly whopping amount—you can plant an acre of turnips or pumpkins with 5 pounds of seed.

Tiny seed goes farther than large seed. For example, it takes ¼ teaspoon of amaranth seed to sow a single row in our standard seedling tray. It takes 2 teaspoons of radish seed to sow a single row. The trouble with buying tiny seed like amaranth or watercress is that a single ounce contains thousands of seeds, more than you could possibly use in even a year's time with numerous succession sowings. Seed packets usually contain the smallest amounts of commercially available seed, so if packets are available for the varieties you want to grow, they may be your best way to start out.

I recommend that you pre-soak large seed such as pea, corn, and sunflower to soften the seed hulls and accelerate germination. Simply place seed in a bowl, fill with room-temperature water, and allow it to soak overnight, before draining and sowing.

Pre-soaking will also promote a more uniform growth pattern in plants once they have sprouted. Wheatgrass, a microgreen grown primarily for use in a nutrient-rich beverage of the same name, can be harvested in greater volume when pre-soaking has ensured more even growth across the entire seedbed. That means more wheatgrass to add to the juicing machine.

Pre-soaking tiny seed in this way, however, just invites problems. The trouble is, small seed tends to clump together when retrieved from water and becomes more difficult to distribute evenly. My father always added fine sand to begonia seed, which is tinier than tiny, when he was growing that bedding plant commercially. The sand increased the palpable size and volume of the seed, making it easier to sow evenly.

The same trick can be applied to handling tiny microgreen seed varieties such as red-veined sorrel, amaranth, and watercress. Simply place a small amount of sand (sterilized play sand) in a paper cup, add the micro seed, and mix thoroughly. Now you're ready to sow seed without worrying about oversowing.

Like many purveyors, Johnny's Selected Seeds sells its seed by the pound, including the ¼-pound amounts that I recommend first-time gardeners start with. If seed is stored in a cool, dry place to avoid changes in temperature and humidity, it will usually remain viable into a second and even third growing season, but I find that older seed, even if it germinates readily, does not enjoy the same healthy growth found with fresh seed. Sowing succession crops of microgreens at intervals of two to three weeks will consume a good deal of seed in the course of a calendar year. Consider ordering microgreen blends that mix three or four different seed varieties with identical growth rates and patterns. Johnny's, for example, offers a mix of mildly flavored brassicas containing mizuna, cabbage, kale, and kohlrabi, all of which reach harvest stage at the same time.

To help you decide how much seed to order for your first venture in microgreens gardening, we have devised the Microgreens Sowing & Harvest Guide (see chart) for the 50 or so varieties we handle. The guide includes seed amounts per seedling tray, days to germination, growth rates, harvest times, and other practical information.

SOWING SEED

As I mentioned earlier, in our commercial microgreens operation, we sow seed in straight rows in plastic 1020 seedling trays filled with soil. We have fabricated a simple plywood template conforming to the size of the tray with two handles on it that allows us to press evenly across the soil surface to create shallow furrows for receiving the seed. You could fabricate a similar tool for making rows. Or simply cut a pencil-sized dowel to the length of the seedling tray and use the dowel to press into the soil at regular intervals to make the seven rows.

Peter Novajosky

We use a device called a seed vibrator to distribute the seed evenly along the seven furrows. A small paper cup would work just as well for sowing seed in a home operation, whether you sow in rows or in broadcast or scatter-sow style. It will take just a few

Microgreen Sowing & Harvest Guide

Amt Seeds Per Row*	Amt Seeds To Order	Microgreen Variety	Amt For Cluster Sowing**	Days To Germination	Days To Microgreen Size	Days To Petite Edible Size	Days To Baby Green Size***
⅛ tsp	1 oz	Amaranth	¼ tsp	5	16	21	
⅛ tsp	1 oz	Arugula - Roquette	¼ tsp	3	16	21	26
⅛ tsp	1 oz	Basil - Genovese	¼ tsp	6	21	30	
⅛ tsp	1 oz	Basil - Lemon	¼ tsp	6	24	34	
⅛ tsp	1 oz	Basil - Lime	¼ tsp	8	28	40	
⅛ tsp	1 oz	Basil - Red Ruben	¼ tsp	6	21	30	
⅛ tsp	1 oz	Basil - Thai	¼ tsp	8	24	34	
1 tsp	2 oz	Beets	1½ tsp	5	18	24	34
⅛ tsp	1 oz	Black Cumin	¼ tsp	10	24	32	
¼ tsp	1 oz	Broccoli	⅜ tsp	5	10	18	26
⅛ tsp	1 oz	Bronze Fennel	¼ tsp	6	21	38	
¼ tsp	1 oz	Cabbage	⅜ tsp	6	10	18	
¹⁄₁₆ tsp	1 oz	Carrots	⅛ tsp	10	30	40	
¹⁄₁₆ tsp	1 oz	Celery	⅛ tsp	14	36	45	
¼ tsp	1 oz	Chervil	¼ tsp	6	20	24	
¼ tsp	1 oz	Chives - Garlic	½ tsp	10	24	36	
1 tsp	2 oz	Cilantro	1½ tsp	6	18	24	
¹⁄₁₆ tsp	1 oz	Claytonia	⅛ tsp	10	24	32	
⅛ tsp	1 oz	Clover	¼ tsp	10	18	28	
¼ tsp	1 oz	Collard Greens	½ tsp	5	16	20	

Amt Seeds Per Row*	Amt Seeds To Order	Microgreen Variety	Amt For Cluster Sowing**	Days To Germination	Days To Microgreen Size	Days To Petite Edible Size	Days To Baby Green Size***
2 tsp	4 oz	Corn Shoots	1 TBS	7	14	16	
⅛ tsp	1 oz	Cress - Cressida	¼ tsp	3	14	20	
¼ tsp	1 oz	Dill	½ tsp	7	21	28	
⅛ tsp	1 oz	Endive - Rhodus	¼ tsp	6	14	18	21
⅛ tsp	1 oz	Fenugreek	¼ tsp	10	24	30	
⅛ tsp	1 oz	Flax	¼ tsp	7	21	28	
¼ tsp	1 oz	Kale - Red Russian	⅜ tsp	5	14	20	
¼ tsp	1 oz	Kohlrabi	⅜ tsp	5	12	18	26
⅛ tsp	1 oz	Lemongrass	¼ tsp	14	36	48	
⅛ tsp	1 oz	Lettuce - Wildfire	¼ tsp	6	14	20	26
⅛ tsp	1 oz	Lettuce - Green Salad Bowl	¼ tsp	6	14	20	24
⅛ tsp	1 oz	Lettuce - Red Lollo	¼ tsp	6	14	20	24
⅛ tsp	1 oz	Lettuce - Romaine Red	¼ tsp	7	16	21	24
¼ tsp	1 oz	Lovage	½ tsp	10	28	40	
¼ tsp	1 oz	Mache	½ tsp	7	21	34	
⅛ tsp	1 oz	Mesclun	¼ tsp	5	12	21	26
¼ tsp	1 oz	Mexican Tarragon	½ tsp	7	21	34	
⅛ tsp	1 oz	Mizuna	¼ tsp	5	12	18	

Amt Seeds Per Row*	Amt Seeds To Order	Microgreen Variety	Amt For Cluster Sowing**	Days To Germination	Days To Microgreen Size	Days To Petite Edible Size	Days To Baby Green Size***
⅛ tsp	1 oz	Mustard	¼ tsp	5	12	18	
1 TBS	4 oz	Nasturtium	2 TBS	7	14	18	
⅛ tsp	1 oz	Pac Choi	¼ tsp	6	12	18	
⅛ tsp	1 oz	Parsley	¼ tsp	10	24	36	
No	4 oz	Pea Shoots	1 oz	6	14	16	
¹⁄₁₆ tsp	1 oz	Purslane	⅛ tsp	6	28	40	
½ tsp	2 oz	Radish - Red Rambo	1 tsp	5	12	18	
½ tsp	1 oz	Salad Burnet	1 tsp	7	20	30	
¼ tsp	1 oz	Saltwort	½ tsp	8	24	36	
¼ tsp	1 oz	Scallions	½ tsp	8	24	36	
⅛ tsp	1 oz	Shungiku	¼ tsp	5	12	18	
¹⁄₁₆ tsp	1 oz	Sorrel	⅛ tsp	7	18	24	
¹⁄₁₆ tsp	1 oz	Sorrel -Red-Veined	⅛ tsp	10	28	45	
¼ tsp	4 oz	Spinach	½ tsp	6	20	26	34
No	4 oz	Sunflower Shoots	1 oz	5	12	16	
½ tsp	2 oz	Swiss Chard	¾ tsp	7	18	24	34
¹⁄₁₆ tsp	4 oz	Watercress	⅛ tsp	3	14	20	
No	1 oz	Wheatgrass	1 oz	7	12	14	
⅛ tsp	1 oz	Yukina Savoy	¼ tsp	5	12	18	

* Amount of seed needed to sow on 20" row in a standard 1020 sowing tray (accommodating 7 rows in total).

** Amount of seed needed to cluster-sow one 5½" square berry box (8 of which fit in a standard 1020 sowing tray).

*** Not all microgreens are edible or desirable at baby green size; when no days are indicated, it means that variety is best harvested either at Microgreen or Petite Edible stage.

repetitions to get the technique down pat—"it's all in the wrist." Where you have sprinkled seed a bit thickly, spread the seed out with a plastic fork, using a raking motion. Add sprinkles of seed in any thin spots. Relatively large seeds such as beets, peas, and wheatgrass are easier to scatter sow than the many tiny seed varieties. Generally, we prefer row sowing because it provides better control both in sowing and harvesting, but if you have a steady hand, you can sow seed either way.

WATERING

Once trays are sown, water seed with a gentle spray using a watering can or mister. Cover each seed bed with a double layer of cheesecloth cut to the dimensions of your planting containers. During the several days before germination, it is important to keep seed moist, and the protective cheesecloth covers will help that. Water gently but thoroughly through the covers, which are porous. Remove the covering when shoots appear. At this point begin testing the soil's moisture level with your finger before deciding when to water again, and do so at the base of the plants to discourage mold or fungus.

Paper towels can be substituted for the cheesecloth, but with repeated waterings the paper will deteriorate, and it may be in shreds by the time you're ready to remove it after plants have germinated. Be sure to keep the towels moist, watering from the top, for if they dry out they will start absorbing moisture from the soil bed, which defeats the whole purpose of covering a seedbed to keep it moist. Cheesecloth has the advantage of being lighter than paper towels when moistened, and we recommend it for this purpose.

Keep soil moist until germination occurs. Moisture levels are not as critical after seeds have germinated, but tiny seedlings still need to drink. While direct sunlight is generally good for plants at this stage of growth, too much heat can dry out the soil bed completely, halting or impeding growth. Conditions in the house, particularly room temperature and exposure to sunlight, will determine how quickly or how slowly the soil bed in your seedling trays dry out.

Here is a trick we use in our greenhouses to stay on top of the need for watering. We lift trays one after another off the benches to gauge the weight of each tray in our hands. If a tray feels too light, it means it needs to be watered. If you do this with your own trays on a daily basis, you will quickly develop a feel for when a seedling tray feels too light, or just right.

A good general rule for watering, indoors or outside, is to do it first thing in the morning.

Here's an important maintenance tip. Every three or four weeks, give the holding trays containing your seedling trays a thorough cleaning. No matter how judiciously you water your plants, fungus can develop in the trays used to disperse excess moisture. Temporarily remove the seedling tray and take the holding tray to the kitchen sink. Dump the pebbles lining the tray in a sieve or other container and wash with a mild detergent, then rinse. Or use a mixture of household bleach, one part bleach to nine parts water. Scrub down the tray itself with the cleansing solution, rinse, and replace the pebbles. Return the tray to its station and restore the seedling tray.

HARVESTING

Microgreens are ready to harvest when they have reached a height of 1½ to 2 inches, approximately two to four weeks after sowing. For some varieties, like radishes and kale, this will be when the seed leaves called cotyledons have fully developed. For other varieties, like coriander and peas, it will coincide with the appearance of the first true leaves produced by the plant itself. See our Microgreens Sowing & Harvest Guide for approximate harvest dates for each microgreen variety at several stages of growth.

Well-sharpened scissors or cutting knives are important for the harvest, as they greatly reduce tissue bruising and the crushing of stems. Cut near the soil to obtain as much volume as you can. If portions of the crop are left for harvest a day or two later, make sure any loose cuttings are removed from the soil bed, as such debris may invite problems like mold and rot. We use a small, hand-held vacuum cleaner of the kind used for cleaning car interiors for this task and it leaves our seed beds in pristine condition. The home gardener can keep his or her micros debris-free by gently raking between the rows of seedlings with a kitchen fork or other suitable instrument.

The harvest can be used immediately in recipes or stored in a refrigerator in plastic bags or other suitable containers for up to 10 days.

Whether or not you should wash microgreens after harvesting them depends on the circumstances. If you harvest your greens with such surgical precision that no soil gets on the stems or leaves, you may not need to rinse them off. My wife, Marie, however, is of the opinion that a single grain of dust or dirt will spoil her salad, so she gives her microgreens a quick rinse using a salad spinner.

In any event, don't wash your greens if you're going to store them for

Peter Novajosky

more than a day. Microgreens will deteriorate faster in storage when wet. So wash if you must—but only just prior to use.

MULTIPLE CUTTINGS

Some microgreens, such as chive, lemongrass, lovage, and parsley, lend themselves to multiple harvests. In other words, after you have made your first cutting, let the crop regroup, recover, and produce new growth until it is tall enough to harvest again. To sustain such prolonged growth, it's important to replenish the seedbed with nutrients. Feed your greens at about two-week intervals, using an organic liquid fertilizer such as fish emulsion or kelp.

POST HARVEST

When a crop has completed its growing cycle and has been fully harvested, it is time to dispose of the soil. Recycle soil in a compost bin or compost pile, roots and all. Or incorporate it directly into any garden soil you may have access to. It will make a welcome organic additive in the garden. Wash for reuse berry boxes and any other containers you have used, or replace with new containers. Sterilize plastic holding trays and seedling trays with a mild detergent or bleach-and-water mix solution so that they are ready for reuse.

Microgreen Varieties at a Glance

Here are the growth rates and growing habits of the more than 50 microgreen varieties we cultivate at Gilbertie's, along with the history, culinary uses, and reported nutritional values of each green.

AMARANTH *AMARANTHUS CAUDATUS*

Amaranth is an attractive-looking annual that does best in the heat of summer when soil is at least 68 degrees Fahrenheit. It was once a major grain crop for many of the peoples of Central and South America and is making a comeback as a food staple because it is rich in protein, iron, calcium, and Vitamins A and C.

As a microgreen it's popular with chefs because of its striking dark-burgundy stems and fuschia-tinged leaves. (Other varieties are predominantly green with red and white stripes.) The young leaves are tender and have a delicate, earthy flavor.

The red variety is so much in demand that it has become more difficult to locate suppliers of certifiably organic and untreated seed, so we grow a crop in one of our fields just to harvest the seed for use in our greenhouses.

Amaranth seed germinates in three to four days when soil temperature is 60 degrees Fahrenheit or higher. Harvest when plant produces cotyledon leaves in 8 days, true leaves in 12 days, or baby leaves in 20–25 days.

Keep soil relatively drier for amaranth than for most microgreens, especially after germination, as it thrives in dry and warm conditions. Overwatering is a no-no.

Peter Novajosky

Called Chinese spinach, amaranth is cut and steamed in Asian cuisines as well as strewn raw in salads.

Amaranth is a bit more challenging to grow in the winter months than many other microgreens, but its coloration and flavor make it worth the effort.

ARUGULA *ERUCA SATIVA*

Also known as rocket or roquette, arugula is a longtime favorite among Italian gardeners and really came into its own in the U.S. in the 1990s. In the garden it seems to germinate the moment you turn your back on it after sowing. The same is true with growing it as a microgreen—in most cases you'll have a micro crop in 7 to 10 days. It will take about two weeks for the plant to reach petite size, and three to four weeks to reach baby leaf size.

When growing to the baby leaf stage indoors, it's a good idea to feed the crop with an organic liquid fertilizer, such as fish emulsion, at two weeks. Otherwise the bottom leaves of the plant, having run out of nitrogen, will begin to turn yellow.

Arugula's small, lobed leaves are medium green in color and nut-flavored and peppery to the tongue. The younger the leaves, the spicier the taste. During warm weather the flavor becomes even stronger. Even though arugula stems are slender (and subject to falling over temporarily when watered too aggressively), the crop itself yields a high volume per sowing tray—as much as 6 ounces at the petite size.

Arugula leaves can stand on their own as a salad, and they are equally

Peter Novajosky

good added to other greens as an accent flavor. If you believe everything you read in old herbals, arugula is both an aphrodisiac and a cure for freckles, but I'm not sure which outcome comes first. Medical researchers claim the salad green is rich in vitamins and numerous trace elements.

BASIL *OCIMUM BASILICUM*

There are numerous varieties of this ancient and beloved culinary herb, some of which are well suited for growing as microgreens even though they are very slow to germinate, because micro basil is fairly intense in flavor. Soil temperature from 70 to 75 degrees Fahrenheit may be needed for timely emergence, so definitely treat all basils as hot-weather crops. Figure on at least five days for sprouts of Genovese basil, the popular green-leafed variety often favored for making pesto, to appear from the time of sowing, and two to three weeks for the plants to grow out to a full petite size. In the winter it will take six to seven weeks to reach the harvest stage. If you put artificial grow lights on the crop for 16 hours a day, you can reduce the growing time by a week or two.

Peter Novajosky

Red Ruben has succeeded Dark Opal as the best of the purple basils, with deep iridescent purple leaves and a full basil aroma and flavor, a favorite additive for salads, pizza, and pasta dishes. But this variety is so difficult to grow in winter months that it's not worth it. Wait until mid-February to sow a crop of purple basil.

Both lemon and lime basil can be grown indoors in the winter. Lemon basil has dark green leaves and a distinctive lemon scent. The very best variety, for leaf size and flavor, is called Mrs. Burns. Lime basil has brighter green coloration and a clean, lime scent. The distinct citrus flavor of lemon and lime basil microgreens adds a fresh bite to salads and other dishes. The citrus basils are also a great garnish for Bloody Marys and screwdrivers.

Thai basil combines the traditional clove flavor of basil with a unique sweet undertone. Cinnamon basil, as the name suggests, has a spicy cinnamon flavor. Both varieties are found in many recipes in Indian and Asian cuisines.

Most basil varieties grow fairly close to the soil line, so use precision when cutting them for harvest. Basil bruises easily because it is so tender, so care must also be taken in handling and packing it. Leaves may blacken if you refrigerate basil at too low a temperature, rendering it unusable.

Basil may not be a cure for warts, as early sages believed, but it does have health benefits, including evidence of antioxidant and anti-inflammatory properties. In Italian culture it is regarded as a symbol of love, which in itself makes the herb medicinal in my book.

BEETS *BETA VULGARIS*

Beets, known as blood turnips in earlier times, are members of the amaranth family. Bull's Blood, the American heirloom variety we grow, has deep green leaves and bright red stems, so it's important to harvest the microgreen close to soil level to get the most of its vibrant color. The splash of red is as welcome in salads as the green's earthy

Peter Novajosky

taste. (Other varieties feature bright yellow stems.) Beet micros make a festive garnish for many other dishes, too.

Beet seeds, which look like tiny meteorites, should be pressed into the soil at sowing time to be sure the seed is completely covered. It takes four to six days to germinate. Go easy on watering as beet microgreens are susceptible to rot. Wait until seed hulls drop off plants before harvesting at the petite stage, which usually occurs in 10 to 14 days. A baby leaf crop takes even longer—three to four weeks—but by then the beet greens are not as tender or palatable. You will be better off skipping the late stage and starting a new beet crop instead.

Like many microgreens, beets are a proven antioxidant and rich in vitamins A and B.

BLACK CUMIN *NIGELLA SATIVA*

This is one of the more unusual plants we grow. In fact it is so hard to find certified organic seed for it that we have to import it from Europe. It is a member of the buttercup family, and not to be confused, botanically, with the cumin that is so popular

as a seasoning in Indian, Middle Eastern, and Mexican cuisine and one of the main ingredients in curry. That cumin (*Cuminum cyminum*) is a member of the parsley family, an aromatic spice with a distinctive nutty, peppery flavor. Black cumin resembles caraway in aroma and flavor. It has also been described as "peppery nutmeg."

Black cumin is considered one of the most powerful medicinal plants of all

Peter Novajosky

time. It was found sealed in King Tut's tomb. Mohammed is said to have called black cumin "the remedy for everything but death." Reportedly, there are more than 400 scientific studies backing up its claims as a healing agent for whatever ails you.

It is best to sow black cumin in rows. It germinates in 10 to 14 days, and can be harvested as a microgreen in 28 to 30 days, when it reaches 2–3 inches in height, and as a petite edible crop in 6 weeks, when it is about 4 inches high.

BROCCOLI *BRASSICA OLERACEA*

President George H. W. Bush famously disliked broccoli, but it is one of the nutritional stars of the microgreens family, rich in fiber, minerals, and Vitamins A and C. All the brassicas are believed to possess potent cancer-fighting properties.

One of the easiest microgreens to grow, broccoli should be sown fairly thickly to ensure a full harvest. Germination occurs in just three to four days, and the harvest should begin in 10 to 12 days. Its green leaves are petite and heart-shaped; stems are a pale green-white. Don't wait too long to cut the crop because bottom leaves may start to turn yellow.

Broccoli originated in Italy. American kids call the full-sized vegetable "trees" when it's served on their plate. But its name actually stems from the Italian word for arm, *braccio*.

Broccoli greens are delicious but there's a difference of opinion as to flavor. Some say young shoots taste like mature broccoli, while others detect a more cabbage-like flavor. Either way this microgreen is a treat to grow and to eat.

Peter Novajosky

Peter Novajosky

BRONZE FENNEL *FOENICULUM VULGARE RUBRUM*

A venerable Italian herb called *finocchio*, this bronze variant of the standard green fennel has metallic dark-brown foliage and is grown primarily for its decorative value, but it too has an anise or licorice flavor that can be used in salads and oily fish courses. In the full-grown plant, the seeds, leaves, flower heads, and stems are all used in cooking.

As a microgreen, bronze fennel is slow to germinate and takes around three weeks before its greens are ready to harvest. If the harvest is delayed a few days, the plant's leaves develop in an even more attractive, feathery pattern that adds to its appeal as a garnish or salad ingredient.

Traditional healers prescribe fennel for its diuretic properties and as an aid to digestion.

CABBAGE *BRASSICA OLERACEA*

Another easy-to-grow brassica, the red cabbage cultivar is popular because of its dark purple leaves, veined with red, and dark red stems. It germinates in three to five days, provides a pleasant, mild cabbage flavor, and works well in salads mixed with cousins such as broccoli and kale. Harvest on the early side, in 7 to 10 days, for a sweeter taste and more tender crunch. Cabbage microgreens will yield as much as 6 ounces of edible greens per sowing tray.

Long valued for its healing properties, cabbage helps balance hormones, fights cancer and heart disease, and contains Vitamin C. It was fed to sailors on long voyages to prevent scurvy. In Ancient Rome, it was considered a cure for hangovers.

CARROTS *DAUCUS CAROTA* VAR. *SATIVUS*

Peter Novajosky

Carrots are in demand as a microgreen because of their pretty, ferny tops and not their trademark roots, which do not start to form until four to five weeks of growth. Slow to germinate (8 to 10 days), carrot tops can be cut at 3 to 4 inches high as a micro crop in 21 to 28 days, and as a petite edible in 36 days.

Well known for its health benefits, the carrot is indeed good for the eyes, as advertised, thanks to its vitamin A, and for the skin as well. It contains valuable amounts of antioxidants and is believed to be a good nutritional weapon against cancer, heart disease, and stroke.

The fern-like leaves of this microgreen allow chefs to add delicate carrot flavor to salads without the crunch of julienned carrots.

CELERY *APIUM GRAVEOLENS* VAR. *DULCE*

This underappreciated vegetable is a staple in many soups and an important base flavor in French mirepoix and also in Cajun and Creole cooking. Yet when most of us think of celery, we think of tuna fish salad.

In microgreen circles it is known as "cutting celery" and valued for the distinct celery flavor in its slender stems and delicate, light-green leaves the size of quarters. As a young crop it looks a lot like a delicate version of coriander.

Peter Novajosky

Peter Novajosky

Celery should be sown in rows. It germinates in about 10 to 12 days. Allow it to develop until it reaches its true leaf stage and a height of 3 to 4 inches. Harvest as a microgreen in four weeks, and as a petite edible in five to six weeks.

It's a long time coming, but the flavor and daintiness of cutting celery is worth the wait.

CHERVIL *ANTHRISCUS CEREFOLIUM*

Chervil, parsley, thyme, and tarragon comprise the famous *fines herbes* of French cooking. Chervil has an unusual anise-tarragon flavor that combines particularly well with eggs, vegetables, and salads.

The best way to sow chervil is in rows, because the plant spreads as it grows. Scatter sowing is likely to produce a tangled crop that is harder to cut. Harvest in 14 to 18 days for a micro crop, and three to four weeks for the petite size.

Chervil microgreens have the mild licorice flavor of the mature herb plant and are loaded with vitamins. The fern-like leaf structure is delicate and calls for fastidious watering and harvesting techniques.

CHIVES—GARLIC *ALLIUM TUBEROSUM*

The smallest plant in the onion family, chives are available in numerous varieties. They are native to the Orient and were commonly found in European herb gardens by the sixteenth century. Long valued for their health benefits, chives are rich in iron, calcium, and vitamins A and C, and are credited with reducing cholesterol levels.

Our favorite micro chive to grow is garlic chives, because the tiny shoots have a mild garlic flavor. More than a pretty garnish, they add piquancy to salads, soups, omelets, and various meat and fish dishes.

Garlic chives take their time to germinate; you may have to wait 10 days for it to happen and four weeks or more before they reach harvest stage at 2 inches in height. We sow the tiny seed at a fairly heavy rate—2 tablespoons of seed per sowing tray.

Be sure to plant chives in straight rows to facilitate successive harvests. It is one of the few microgreen crops that can be left to grow again and again, with the opportunity for as many as four to six harvests. To help foster this additional bounty, fertilize with fish emulsion or liquid seaweed at two-week intervals.

A good rule to follow for garlic chives and for any other micro crop that permits multiple cuttings is to clean up the seed bed following each and every harvest. Bits and pieces of stems and shoots fall to the bottom of the sowing tray even with the most surgical of harvests, and left in place this residue, especially if it becomes moist, can cause rot and fungus. The cleanup can be accomplished by hand or with the help of a kitchen fork.

Peter Novajosky

Peter Novajosky

CILANTRO *CORIANDRUM SATIVUM*

The botanical name for this microgreen, coriander, comes from *koris*, the Greek word for bedbug. This less-than-glamorous association is explained by the herb's unusual fragrance, a combination of sage and citrus flavors that some people find unpleasant. Indeed, it is one of the "bitter herbs" brought to the table by Jewish families as they observe Passover. Yet its leaves and seeds are highly valued in many of the world's cuisines, including Mexican, Thai, and Indian.

Not one of the easiest microgreens to cultivate, cilantro takes five to seven days to germinate and is not ready to harvest until almost three weeks. Grow the green until it reaches the true leaf stage for best flavor. Chefs tend to use it independently of other greens because its unique aroma and taste can be overwhelming.

One of the oldest herbs known to humankind, cilantro is credited with numerous medical properties as well as its many culinary uses. The seed produced by cilantro is generally labeled coriander in spice racks, and often has different applications in recipes.

CLAYTONIA *CLAYTONIA PERFOLIATA*

This cold-hardy salad green forms pairs of heart-shaped leaves around white-flowered stems. It flowers more quickly than any other microgreen we grow. If we miss harvesting a few plants in the seedling trays, they will drop seed, and several weeks later we find ourselves harvesting claytonia off the greenhouse floor.

For all that bother, claytonia is well worth growing because the flavor of its young leaves is wild and fresh. Also, you can get several cuttings from one crop, and for that reason it should be sown in straight rows. Allow eight days for claytonia to germinate. It will reach microgreen size in 18 days and petite size in 25 days.

Peter Novajosky

CLOVER *TRIFOLIUM PRATENSE*

This familiar roadside attraction is best known as a cover crop for improving the nitrogen content of soil and as a reliable source of animal fodder. A member of the pea family, clover has a crisp texture and nutty flavor that makes it palatable to man and beast alike. We grow the red variety as a microgreen, but white clover (*Trifolium repens*) is widely cultivated as well.

Clover takes 7 to 10 days to germinate and can be harvested as a micro in 20 to 28 days, and as a petite edible in 36 to 40 days. Highly nutritious, it's a favorite for mixing with other salad greens and as a crunchy topping for sandwichs or wraps.

Normally, clover produces three leaves on a delicate stem, but once in a while a four-leaf clover, or shamrock, will appear. I have never found a shamrock in my life, but I have a neighbor who routinely comes upon them and stops by to show me his prize every time. Of course, he would be Irish.

COLLARD GREENS *BRASSICA OLERACEA*

Like kohlrabi, humble collards are enjoying a new career as a highly desirable micro-green. A staple in southern U.S. cuisine, the plant grows to about 2 feet in height

Peter Novajosky

and produces large dark leaves. It is eaten on New Year's Day in Dixie, along with black-eyed peas and cornbread, for good luck. (Because its leaves resemble folding money, feasting on this slightly bitter green is said to ensure greater wealth in the coming year—a cash crop if there ever was one.)

Collard greens germinate in four to five days and reach a micro height of 2 inches in 14 days. Harvest them as petite edibles in 20 days, and as baby greens in 28 to 30 days.

The health benefits of collards have been well documented: they are a good source of vitamins C and K and of other nutrients with anticancer properties.

CORN SHOOTS *ZEA MAYS*

Sweet corn and the various commercial popcorn varieties, with somewhat smaller seed, can all be grown as microgreen shoots with quick and satisfying results. Pre-soaking seed for 24 hours before sowing will accelerate germination and allow plants to grow at the same rate. Once corn shoots have appeared, most growers cover them with dark plastic or some other suitable material to create a blanching effect,

Peter Novajosky

a process that takes about a week. Easier still, take an empty sowing tray, turn it upside down, and cover the fledgling crop with it.

Blanching imbues the shoots with an attractive yellow color that is fun to add to salads. If the crop is prematurely exposed to light, you might be surprised how quickly photosynthesis turns the shoots back to green. Allow two weeks before harvesting.

As with pea shoots, corn shoots can be refrigerated to keep their freshness for up to a week. The shoots are sweet and tender to the taste—just plain a-maize-ing, if you can stand the pun.

CRESS *LEPIDIUM SATIVUM*

Garden cress is easy to grow as a microgreen. Its tiny, tender leaves develop on a white stem and have a tangy flavor and satisfying bite. It is the key ingredient in the classic English egg sandwich undoubtedly served at high tea every day on TV's *Downton Abbey*. It is also good atop salads, hummus spreads, and other vegetable side dishes. Although its shelf life is short, because it is so delicate, a little goes a long way.

Peter Novajosky

There are several varieties of cress. We've had the most success with Cressida, known as curly cress for its curled leaves, and Wrinkled Crinkled Cress, which has fancy crinkled leaves. Both germinate in as early as three days. Harvest within 8 to 10 days to make sure you obtain this microgreen, a member of the mustard family, at its peppery best.

Garden cress is not to be confused with another very piquant green, water-cress, which is actually in the nasturtium family and takes quite special conditions to flourish. It grows in shallow, fresh running water in spots protected from surges of water which could disrupt the plantings.

The health benefits claimed for cress over the ages are many and diverse, including stimulating the appetite, preventing hair loss, and improving one's sex life. Take your pick!

DILL *ANETHUM GRAVEOLENS*

One of our most popular culinary herbs, dill comes in three sizes. The tallest, at 3 to 4 feet high, is the variety that held a place of honor in the gardens of ancient Greece and Rome. It is still coveted by today's gardeners for its towering presence. The more compact-growing Dill Bouquet, topping off at 30 inches, is ideal for gardens where space is at a premium. It's just as elegant as its big sister and provides more than enough useful clippings for the home chef. Then there's Fernleaf Dill, with its even neater growing habit and attractive dark-green foliage.

Peter Novajosky

As a microgreen, all three dill varieties produce feathery leaves with that distinctive dill aroma and flavor that pairs so admirably with egg dishes, cucumbers, potatoes, and many kinds of fish dishes, especially salmon. The big difference is in the cost of seed: Fernleaf Dill is 20 times more expensive than the other two kinds.

Fortunately, dill seed for microgreens is available at quite reasonable prices, and it's the kind we grow for market.

It is better to plant dill in straight rows, rather than cluster sowing, because it will be easier to harvest as a row crop. Dill germinates readily in 6 to 7 days and is ready to cut as a micro/petite crop in 14 to 18 days, when it is 3 to 4 inches high. It doesn't lend itself to multiple cuttings, but surplus harvests will keep well if properly packed and refrigerated.

ENDIVE *CICHORIUM ENDIVIA* 'RHODUS'

Also known as curly endive, or frisée, for the jagged or serrated edges of its leaves, this green is not to be confused with Belgian endive, which is a cultivated variety of common chicory, or with its cousin escarole, which has broader, dark-green leaves.

Peter Novajosky

Endive is crisp in texture and pleasantly bitter in flavor. If allowed to mature into late fall in the garden, its center leaves blanch and it develops a sweeter taste. For eating, endive can be sautéed, chopped into stews or soups, or mixed into a green salad. Nutritionists report that endive is high in fiber and rich in vitamins and minerals.

Endive germinates in 4 to 6 days. Harvest as a micro in 14 to 18 days, as a petite edible in 21 to 26 days, or as a baby green in 35 days. The desired crinkly appearance of the leaves is present at every stage of growth.

FENUGREEK *TRIGONELLA FOENUM-GRAECUM*

In translation, the word for this succulent annual herb of Mediterranean origin means "Greek hay." Its seeds, small, hard, and oval shaped, are commonly used in Indian cooking; the plant's small, light-green leaves are one of the basic ingredients for making curry. There are various age-old medicinal uses for fenugreek but the FDA has not yet weighed in on their efficacy.

Not the easiest micro for growing at home, fenugreek's seed takes seven days to germinate, and growth is correspondingly slow. The plant reaches a micro height of 3 to 4 inches in three weeks, and a petite edible height of 4 to 5 inches in four weeks.

Fenugreek has a bittersweet flavor, akin to celery or lovage, and a crunchy texture. It can be eaten raw or cooked. As a micro it is probably most popular as a zesty addition to mixed green salads.

FLAX *LINUM USITATISSIMUM*

The Latin name for flax means "most useful," and that certainly applies to this plant long cultivated as a food and fiber crop, from the eastern Mediterranean into India and to western Asia. An annual, it grows 3 to 4 feet high, producing green leaves on slender stems and beautiful blue or red five-petal flowers in the fall.

It is the tough fiber from the plant's stems that is used to manufacture linen. An important byproduct of flax seed is linseed oil, of which Canada, incidentally, is the world's leading provider. Flax seed is also an edible source of fiber, with high levels of vitamins, minerals, and antioxidants, as well.

For microgreens, flax seed germinates in five to seven days. Harvest a week later when the greens are 2 inches high. Leaves have a spicy flavor that add welcome bite to salads.

KALE *BRASSICA OLERACEA ACEPHALA* 'RED RUSSIAN'

Medical researchers have determined that one cup of kale provides 134 percent of an average adult's daily requirement of vitamin C, 206 percent of vitamin A, and 684 percent of vitamin K. No wonder kale is called the queen of greens.

Peter Novajosky

This leafy garden vegetable, once a staple of World War II victory gardens, has made a comeback in recent times, in part because of its newly discovered nutritional value. Kale now takes center stage on menus in five-star restaurants and in recipes on cooking shows and in the food sections of magazines and newspapers. It can be enjoyed raw or cooked.

Mature kale is a popular late-fall and early-winter vegetable because it becomes sweeter and more flavorful after a freeze. In Ireland and Holland, it is often chopped up, cooked, and added to mashed potatoes. Tender kale microgreens make an intense addition to salads. Kale is often combined with broccoli and cabbage micros to make a salad mix with bite and contrasting colors.

Easy to grow, especially in cool temperatures, Red Russian micro kale has tiny green leaves similar to clover, purplish-red stems, and a thick, low-growing habit that provides excellent yields. Germination takes three to five days. Harvest as a microgreen in about 14 days, as a petite edible in 18 days, and as a baby green in about four weeks.

Peter Novajosky

KOHLRABI *BRASSICA OLERACEA* 'PURPLE VIENNA'

At maturity, the garden vegetable kohlrabi looks like a stereo headset worn by a Martian. Its grown for the bulblike formation that develops just above the soil line, from which slender stems sprout like so many antennas. Behind this comical façade, however, lies a versatile food crop with a crisp texture and delicate, sweet taste. Edible raw or cooked, its German name means "cabbage turnip," and it is a staple in the cuisines of countries as different as Hungary and India.

Kohlrabi is enjoying newfound fame as a microgreen because it adds so much texture, flavor, and visual flair to salads and stir-fries. Its cultivation is similar to that of kale. Germination occurs in three to five days even in cool soil conditions as low as 50 to 60 degrees Fahrenheit. Water the crop evenly and thoroughly whenever the soil bed feels dry. Harvest when it reaches 3 to 4 inches in height, about 10 to 14 days for a micro crop, 18 days for petite. Don't let it grow into baby leaves, as it starts to turn yellow at that stage.

There is an apple-green variety of kohlrabi, but the consensus is that the purple strain tastes better. Nutrition-wise, kohlrabi is high in fiber, calcium, potassium, and vitamins A and C.

LEMONGRASS *CYMBOPOGON FLEXUOSUS*

Native to Sri Lanka and India, this exotic, heat-loving herb forms dense, tall clumps of broad grass blades in the garden; these leaves smell intensely of lemon drops.

There is an Asian variety of lemongrass that forms a bulb-like growth at the bottom of its stem, but it can only be propagated from division. The East Indian variety that grows from seed is the one used to produce lemongrass as a microgreen.

This micro is very difficult to grow from seed, however. To start with, its small, elongated seed is encased in a feathery attachment that must be separated before sowing by rubbing the seed between fingertips. (Occasionally you'll find "clean" seeds without that attachment available from a supplier, which makes the sowing simpler, akin to sowing basil seed.) Lemongrass takes a long time to germinate—at least two weeks. In about six weeks, it is ready to harvest as a 4-inch-high micro. Don't let it get much taller, as it will become too fibrous to enjoy in salads or the many Asian recipes that call for its use.

Plan multiple cuttings of lemongrass to get your money's worth out of this herb, with its strong lemon scent and flavor. After each harvest, tidy up between rows. Feed every two weeks with an organic liquid fertilizer to keep the grass growing.

LETTUCE *LACTUCA SATIVA*

Lettuce is a versatile, easy-to-grow microgreen available in an abundance of colors, shapes, and sizes. Many seed purveyors offer a blend of lettuce varieties with the same germination and growth rate, allowing the home gardener to cultivate several different lettuces in the same seedling tray. My favorite salad mix includes black-seeded Simpson, Red Lollo, red salad bowl, and red and green romaine.

Peter Novajosky

Lettuce germinates in four to five days and is ready to harvest as a microgreen in 14 days, as a petite edible in 21 days, and as baby greens in 28 days. If possible, keep the seedlings on the cool side after germination and they will perform better for you.

It is possible to obtain two or three cuttings from a lettuce micro crop, but extra care must be taken in watering. Seeds are so thickly sown that when they reach 4 inches in height, it is difficult to irrigate the plants without moisture remaining on the base of the leaves (where leaf joins stem), and that invites rot and mold. Take special care to water seedlings at the soil line only.

LOVAGE *LEVISTICUM OFFICINALE*

This venerable English "sweet herb" was once favored for its medicinal attributes, but today is primarily used in candy and other confections. A hardy perennial, it reaches a height of 6 feet in the garden.

As a microgreen, lovage is valued for its celery-like flavor and makes a surprising addition to salads and as a garnish for soups. Easy to grow, it germinates in 10

days. Because it is a floppy grower, we sow lovage in five rows instead of the usual seven, in a standard 10" x 20" seedling tray. It is ready to harvest as a micro in 28 days, and as a petite edible in 35 to 40 days. The ideal height for cutting is 4 to 5 inches. After the first harvest, it will grow back for additional cuttings when fertilized at two-week intervals.

Peter Novajosky

MÂCHE *VALERIANELLA LOCUSTA*

Also known as corn salad or lamb's lettuce, this cool-season green is quite popular in many European countries, enjoyed for its tender leaves and nutty flavor and often served as a stand-alone salad, or mixed with other salad greens.

Peter Novajosky

Mâche poses a challenge for commercial growers because its soft leaves are susceptible to rot and mildew if moisture gets on them. With close supervision, however, especially when watering, this problem can be avoided with homegrown crops.

Mâche seeds germinate in about 5 to 7 days and can be harvested as microgreens in 18 to 20 days, and as petite edibles in 25 to 28 days. Leaves form as rosettes and should be cut in their entirety at the base of the plant. Mâche does not tolerate heat very well, so take it off your summer planting schedule.

MESCLUN

Every grower has his or her favorite blend of mesclun salad greens. The idea is to mix at least four varieties contrasting in color, flavor, and leaf pattern while making sure each of the seed varieties included in the blend will germinate and grow at the same rate.

Peter Novajosky

We usually include eight varieties in our mesclun blend, among them arugula, red and green Salad Bowl lettuce, tatsoi, and red mustard.

Mesclun mixes germinate in 4 to 6 days and are ready to harvest as a micro crop in 14 days, as petite edibles in 18 to 20 days, and as baby greens in about 25 days.

Mesclun is one of the most dependable and popular microgreens you can grow, and it is good for at least two cuttings. Growers report equal success when scatter-sowing mesclun or sowing the seed in rows.

MEXICAN TARRAGON *TAGETES LUCIDA*

This plant has many aliases—mint marigold, yerba anise, Texas tarragon, to name just a few. A good substitute for French tarragon (*Artemisia dracunulus*) in the winter months in southern gardens, it is a tender perennial that thrives in hot, dry climates, growing to 3 feet in height and producing small yellow flowers in the fall. French tarragon is not available as a microgreen because it has to go through a dormant period.

Mexican tarragon was an important medicinal herb in Aztec pharmacology. Its

Peter Novajosky

leaves have the anise/licorice aroma and taste that fanciers of French tarragon enjoy adding to vinegar, egg dishes, and many other recipes. But when true French tarragon becomes available, chefs are quick to sub it in.

Mexican tarragon germinates in 7 to 8 days. It is ready to harvest as a microgreen in 21 to 24 days, as a petite edible in 28 to 30 days, and as a baby green in 42 to 50 days.

MIZUNA *BRASSICA JUNCEA* 'RED CORAL'

Mustard microgreens are easy to grow, fast to germinate (usually, 3 to 5 days), and highly productive, and this Japanese version is no exception. Also known as California peppergrass, mizuna has a sweet, fresh mustard flavor that adds zing to salads and other dishes. It has white stems, bright green cotyledons, and serrated true leaves with a blush of purple.

Peter Novajosky

Mizuna can be harvested as a micro crop in 3 to 5 days, as a petite edible in 14 days, and as a baby leaf crop in 21 days.

MUSTARD *BRASSICA JUNCEA*

The mustards are a microgreen mainstay because they are so easy to germinate, sprouting to life within 3 to 4 days, and they produce hefty yields within 10 to 12 days. For baby leaves, the wait is about 20 days.

Mustard has what might be called a snappy personality, with flavor intensifying with age. The seeds from mature mustard plants are used to make the popular condiment, which explains

Peter Novajosky

the hearty, spicy flavor found in their leaves. Some chefs find the taste akin to horseradish.

We grow mustard varieties with erect white stems and red or green leaves. There is also a strain with purple-tinged frilly leaves and bright green stems. Their piquant flavors makes them a natural in Asian salad mixes and stir-fries. Micro mustard is also a welcome element in meat, poultry, and seafood dishes. Combining mustard and cress for sandwiches is another classic pairing. For so many reasons, this is one microgreen you should include on your crop list.

Like other hot, spicy greens, mustard claims many health benefits. Rich in anti-oxidants, it is said to be a good defense against colon and bladder cancer.

NASTURTIUM *TROPAEOLUM MAJUS*

Nasturtium microgeens are grown for their tender leaves, the size of quarters and a delicate pale-green color, and not flowers, which require lots of summer sun and heat.

Although seeds are large, they don't need to be soaked overnight, as they will germinate in 4 to 6 days. But make sure the seed is covered with soil to a depth of ¾ inch so that all seeds sprout at the same time. You should enjoy equal success whether you sow in rows or in clusters.

Peter Novajosky

Nasturtium germinates in 7 days. The young leaves can be harvested in 15 to 20 days. The leaves have a brisk, nutty flavor that imparts a welcome freshness to salads and sandwich wraps. Sometimes they pack an appreciable afterbite. We include nasturtium micros in our spicy blend salad mix.

Incidentally, we do supply nasturtium flowers to restaurants and farm markets in the summer, when they become available in an abundance of colors. We usually plant up a hundred or more hanging baskets with nasturtiums and we cut luscious mixes of the blooms from them. Those flowers that escape our scissors inevitably set seed, which itself can be collected and used in food dishes as a replacement for capers. The fresh seed has the same tangy flavor as nasturtium leaves.

Nasturtium flowers, which are often used to top off salads in a rainbow of colors, are also edible, tangy to the taste and delicate in texture.

PAC CHOI (BOK CHOY) *BRASSICA RAPA*

Originating in China and now in widespread use throughout Asia, this green has a mild, sweet flavor somewhere between mustard and broccoli. It is frequently added raw to salads, stir-fries, soups, and noodle dishes. Easy to germinate, usually in three to four days, its harvest crop is voluminous compared to many microgreens, yielding as much as 10 ounces per sowing tray.

Pac choi has white stems and spoon-shaped green leaves with delicate red veins. A red variant has dark-red leaves with green undersides. Growing methods and flavors are comparable. The variant's red color gets even redder when exposed to cooler temperatures for several days.

Peter Novajosky

Peter Novajosky

PARSLEY *PETROSELINUM NEAPOLITANUM*

This flat-leafed version of parsley, also known as Italian parsley, is preferred by most chefs because it has more flavor. Micro parsley offers that same distinctive sweet and spicy flavor in its shamrock-shaped leaves.

The trouble with micro parsley is it takes a lot of patience to grow, needing more time to germinate (10 to 14 days, even when seed is pre-soaked) and to reach the true-leaf stage of development.

Sow parsley in rows (seven rows per 10" x 20" sowing tray) for neatness and ease of maintenance and harvest. Feed the crop with an organic liquid fertilizer at two-week intervals. This will allow you to make three to four successive cuttings—parsley is always in demand in our kitchen. Don't forget to clean up the soil bed after every harvest to be sure no clippings are left behind to rot and generate mold or fungus.

Nowadays, generous bunches of Italian parsley can be found in food markets year-round, but don't be deceived by size. Growers sell parsley to stores by weight, oftentimes augmenting growth with doses of chemical fertilizer, which diminishes flavor. That's why it's still worth including this cultivar in your microgreens repertory, after you have mastered the basics, just for that harvest-time quality and taste of this workhorse herb.

PEA SHOOTS *PISUM SATIVUM*

Pea shoots are one of our most popular microgreens, not only because they are so easy to grow, but because they bring a bright, crunchy taste of spring to salads of every kind. One variety of micro peas produces feathery tendrils on its tender shoots early in the growth stage to make the greens even more exotic.

Peter Novajosky

Soak this large seed in water overnight to soften it, then drain. Sow thickly for more bountiful yields—as much as 12 ounces per sowing tray. Seeds germinate in about three to five days. Shoots are ready to harvest when they attain a height of 2 to 3 inches in just a week's time.

Peas like the cooler weather. Grow micro peas in shade or partial shade in the summer to preserve their dark-green color and sweet flavor. Stems become woody if allowed to elongate, so if the crop gets ahead of you, simply cut the shoots higher on the stem. Be mindful of the fact that peas are at the top of the list of free treats among small birds and mice.

One reason peas are found on dining tables the world over is because of their health benefits. They are a good source of carbs and protein and contain vitamins B1, C, niacin, iron, zinc, and magnesium. Just as your mother always said, "Peas are good for you!"

Peter Novajosky

PURSLANE *PORTULACA OLERACEA*

With its tangy flavor and juicy texture, this common garden weed finally gets its due in the kitchen of knowing home chefs. Actually, purslane has been valued as a leafy vegetable in Europe for ages. Its taste has been compared to watercress and spinach. It contains lots of omega-3 fatty acids, which is surprising for something that's not a fish, and it's also rich in vitamins and minerals.

Not bad for a plant with the nickname pigweed! Purslane is also often called moss rose because its mostly prostrate stems are reddish in color. There's a golden purslane variant with bigger leaves, but we grow the one with red stems.

Sow the tiny seeds of purslane in rows. Germination takes about 5 days. Begin to harvest as a micro crop in 21 days, as a petite edible in 28 days. Because of its growing habit, plants won't get much taller than two or three inches, but they should be easy to cut cleanly.

Purslane is an annual, but it self-sows promiscuously, according to the University of Illinois Extension Service, and its seed is so hardy it remains viable for 40 years. So, if purslane has been in your garden, don't think you've seen the last of it. The good news is that, after weeding, you can add it to salads, rice dishes, stir-fries, and soups.

RADISH *RAPHANUS SATIVUS* 'RED RAMBO'

Radishes have always been ranked in the lower reaches of the world of garden vegetables, dwarfed in popularity and prestige by heirloom tomatoes and fancy lettuce mixes. But as a microgreen, the humble radish is a superstar because it is so easy to grow and provides such a welcome tang to whatever foods it is served with.

Peter Novajosky

Micro radish seed germinates in 3 to 4 days, and seedlings are ready to harvest in 8 to 10 days—the earlier the better as far as flavor and texture are concerned. Our most highly favored Red Rambo variety has purple heart-shaped leaves on dark-purple stems. Colors become more vivid in cooler temperatures, and that applies to all the radish types.

Daikon is a radish variety from Asia; as a microgreen it produces soft green leaves on long white stems. It is pretty and peppery and provides a surprisingly potent afterbite. Hong vit is another Asian import; its seed leaves offer a pleasing dark-green contrast to its vivid purple stem. Both should be harvested when they reach about 2 inches in height.

Radish microgreens, rich in vitamins, minerals, and antioxidants, are ranked high on the list with the brassica family for their putative health benefits.

Peter Novajosky

SALAD BURNET *PROTERIUM SANGUISORBA*

Burnet is the first perennial salad herb ready to harvest in the garden in early spring. Its pronounced cucumber flavor makes it a reliable standby for introducing the taste of cukes into winter salads. This is an especially worthy trait given that cucumber itself does not produce a useful microgreen. Cucumber can be grown as such, but the trouble is the sprouts quickly toughen and change flavor within one or two days; it's just not worth the effort.

Salad burnet germinates in six to seven days. We recommend sowing it in straight rows for ease of care and watering. It takes about three weeks to reach the micro stage, four to five weeks for cutting as a petite edible. After that, the plant becomes tough and less desirable as a salad ingredient.

SALTWORT *SALSOLA KALI*

This traditional Japanese culinary herb, also called "land seaweed," has long, slender, crunchy leaves and is rich in vitamins. It's often added raw to salads and sushi dishes. Saltwort germinates in 8 days, and is ready to harvest as a micro in 12 days, as a petite edible in 24 days, and as a baby green in 36 days.

Food writer Barbara Damrosch had kind words for this often neglected green in a story in the *Washington Post*: "Even after cooking, it never becomes an amorphous blob of mystery greens and thereby makes an especially lovely bed on which to set a nice piece of meat or fish."

SCALLIONS *ALLIUM FISTULOSUM*

Also known as green onions, Japanese bunching onions, or Welch onions, scallions add a mild (milder than chives) onion flavor and pleasant crunch to your salads.

Scallions take six to eight days to germinate and can be harvested as a micro crop in four weeks, when they reach a height of 5 inches, or as 7-inch-high petites in six weeks. Fertilize at two-week intervals to ensure bountiful multiple cuttings.

Peter Novajosky

Like other members of the onion family, scallions help to regulate blood sugar, improve the immune system, and encourage the production of good cholesterol. The green tops are rich in vitamin C.

SHUNGIKU *GLEBIONIS CORONARIA*

One of our faster growers, this plant belongs to the chrysanthemum family; in fact, if it were allowed to fully develop, it would produce edible yellow and orange chrysanthemum blooms. Its small, serrated leaves are also similar to the foliage found on flowering chrysanthemums.

Shungiku germinates in three to

Peter Novajosky

five days. For bigger harvests, sow more thickly than other Asian greens, and cut when plants are about 4 to 5 inches tall. This variety takes 14 days to reach micro stage, 18 days for petite, and 24 for baby leaf.

Also known as garland chrysanthemum or chop suey greens, shungiku has a crisp, aromatic, carrot-like flavor. It is rich in carotenoids and potassium. It's found in many recipes for salads, sushi, casseroles, omelets, and Asian-style stews.

I sometimes feed surpluses of this prolific grower, mixed with various other greens, to my rabbits. They must have read the label because, invariably, the rabbits wolf down the shungiku before moving on to the lesser greens.

SORREL *RUMEX SCUTATUS*

Of the two familiar garden varieties of sorrel, the one with red-veined leaves, although two to three times more expensive to buy as seed, is more attractive as a microgreen than the one with all-green leaves. The green variety has a flatter leaf and more upright growing habit. Both kinds deliver that tangy, lemony, even slightly sour flavor so characteristic of this perennial herb. A little goes a long way in salads, soups, and sauces.

Peter Novajosky

The flashier red-veined sorrel is worth the higher seed price in part because it is possible to obtain multiple cuttings from the crop. Sowing its very tiny seed is an exercise in patience, however, made even more difficult by the fact that the seed has a tendency to roll in all directions.

Sow the sorrel in straight rows for ease of harvest. Germination occurs in

5 to 7 days for the green variety and 10 days for the red-veined variety. It is ready for cutting when it reaches 2 to 4 inches in height. It's best not to let the crop grow taller than 4 inches because it becomes tough and less palatable. The microgreen size takes about 14 to 18 days to mature, petite edibles 21 to 28 days. Clean up the soil bed between rows after every harvest. Fertilize every two weeks to ensure an ample harvest.

SPINACH *SPINACIA OLERACEA*

Spinach, a favorite of Catherine de' Medici and Popeye the Sailor Man, has both delectable flavor and high nutrient content. Originally a cool-weather crop, today there are spinach varieties that thrive in the garden from early spring, grow without bolting in the warm months of summer, and thrive again when planted in the fall.

We have been most successful growing the smooth-leaf variety of spinach as a microgreen. Germination occurs in 5 to 7 days and the crop can be cut as a micro in 20 days when it reaches a height of 1 to 1½ inches. The petite edible size of 2 to 2½ inches comes along at 24 days, and the baby leaf size of 4 inches at 30 days.

A recent introduction called Red Kitten is also worth growing as a micro. Its medium green leaves are borne on upright plants and have red veins, making them a standout when mixed into salad blends. Even better, Red Kitten grows 5 to 7 days faster than other varieties.

A familiar garden crop called New Zealand spinach (*Tetragonia expansa*) is not related to spinach but tastes

Peter Novajosky

like spinach and can be used similarly in cooking and in salads. Thriving in warm weather, it comes into its own when the real spinach begins to wane and provides plentiful greens until the first killing frost.

SUNFLOWER SHOOTS *HELIANTHUS ANNUUS*

Sunflower shoots, sometimes called sunnies, have a delicate, nutty flavor and make a tasty addition to salads and other dishes. Be sure to buy the seed marked for "shoots," as some hybrid sunflower seed is quite a bit more expensive—as much as $300 per pound. This is a sturdy grower and shoots are loaded with vitamins and minerals.

Pre-soak sunflower seed overnight to soften the seed casing and encourage early germination and a more uniform growth rate. Broadcast the drained seed evenly over your planting area, water gently but thoroughly, then cover with cheesecloth or an empty flat (turned upside down) to keep the seedbed moist. Remove the cover at the first sign of sprouting, which usually occurs in 5 to 7 days.

Harvest the shoots when they reach 3 to 4 inches in height, in 10 to 14 days.

 Don't let them get much taller than that, as the shoots become tough and lose their pleasant flavor.

SWISS CHARD *BETA VULGARIS*

This nutritious microgreen with a sweet beet/spinach flavor makes a sprightly garnish and a welcome addition to salads with its dark-green leaves and colorful stems, depending on variety. There's a rainbow assortment of chard varieties in hues of red, yellow, orange, white, and purple.

As with beets, make sure the large, knobby seed of chard is fully covered

Peter Novajosky

by soil when sown. It will germinate in about 6 days and be ready for harvest as a microgreen in 12 days. For the petite size, wait 14 to 20 days before cutting.

Historically, chard was cultivated by ancient peoples throughout the Mediterranean region, so I've never been able to figure out how little, landlocked Switzerland gets all the credit for it.

WHEATGRASS *TRITICUM AESTIVUM*

Wheatgrass is different from most microgreens in that it is grown not to be eaten directly but to be dissolved in a juicing machine and consumed as a beverage. It has a pleasant, slightly grassy flavor. Some whatgrass fans blend it with bananas and other fruit to make the elixir even tastier and better for you.

Peter Novajosky

And talk about healthy drinks—stand back, carrot juice! It has been reported that a mere eighth of a cup of wheatgrass juice has as much nutritional value as eating two pounds of leafy green vegetables. Wheatgrass has more vitamin C than orange juice. It has twice the vitamin A of carrots. And it can leap tall buildings in a single bound. No, wait, that's Superman.

Health claims aside, wheatgrass is easy to grow, although it takes longer to reach the volume of growth to make the grain worthwhile to harvest for juicing purposes. That's why it's so important to pre-soak wheatgrass seed overnight before use. The pre-soaking will ensure uniform germination and rate of growth.

Sow micro wheatgrass thickly and wait until shoots reach 4 to 6 inches in height before cutting. This will usually take about 10 to 14 days. Regular watering is a must. If you find the grass is at harvest stage but you are not ready to cut it, place the entire tray in a refrigerator to keep it to size.

With wheatgrass it is impossible to stress too much the importance of growing in organic nutrient-rich soil and of fertilizing with organic nutrients following germination. The goodness in the wheatgrass juice literally comes from the good properties of the soil in which it is grown.

Once it is liquefied, wheatgrass can be refrigerated for up to a week without losing its nutrient value.

YUKINA SAVOY *BRASSICA RAPA*

Asian greens have become a familiar offering at farm markets and in gourmet food stores because their diversity of color, texture, and flavor—ranging from mildly pungent to sweet—invite so many different uses in salads, soups, and stir-fries.

Peter Novajosky

In this category, tatsoi may be familiar to many home chefs, but lately we have preferred growing yukina savoy instead. We've found this variety is a more upright and vigorous grower and holds its dark green color much better than other Asian greens. The "savoy" in the term refers to the distinctive crinkled texture of the leaves, which are fairly large.

Yukina is very easy to grow, germinating in 5 to 7 days. It's ready to harvest at the microgreen stage in 14 days, as a petite in 21 days, and as a baby green in 24 days. After three weeks, it has a tendency to turn yellow in the tray, so make sure you reap what you have sown in a timely fashion.

Frequently Asked Questions About Microgreens

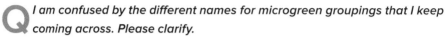 **I am confused by the different names for microgreen groupings that I keep coming across. Please clarify.**

Microgreens are a relatively new phenomenon in the gardening world so it's not surprising some of the terminology is confusing. Broadly speaking, microgreens are the edible shoots and leaves of salad greens, leafy vegetables, herbs, and some flowers. They are sown close together in soil and harvested when still quite small, often within two to three weeks of sowing.

Many professional growers, Gilbertie's Herb Gardens & Petite Edibles included, classify the greens in three size groups. The plants we label "microgreens" are harvested the earliest, when they reach a height of 1½ to 2 inches. "Petite edibles" are harvested at 2 to 3 inches. "Baby greens" are harvested at 3 to 4 inches.

All three size groups are sown, maintained, and harvested in the same way, with some minor differences in growing methods depending on variety. All three size groups can be used interchangeably in salads and other recipe applications.

Although different labels are often used to differentiate among greens depending on harvest size, you would not be amiss or in error to refer to all of them by the generic name of microgreens.

 What's the difference between shoots and sprouts?

Shoots are a common name for certain microgreens. Pea shoots refer to the green tips and tendrils of pea plants. Sunflower and squash shoots are the tender and nutritious offspring of sunflower and squash seed. Wheatgrass shoots are produced by hard red spring wheat, often processed in the blender to make a protein-rich smoothie. Corn and popcorn shoots develop from seed, popcorn being somewhat smaller than standard corn kernels in seed size. Growers like to cover corn shoots in the early growing stages to prevent chlorophyll formation, which gives the shoots a yellowish cast that chefs find desirable for adding to salads.

Unlike microgreen shoots, all of which are grown in soil, sprouts are not grown in a planting medium. They germinate in water, in low light, from the seeds of greens or grains and are eaten, as immature seedlings, roots and all, most often in salads and on sandwiches. Food safety is a greater issue with sprouts than with microgreens, so it is important to follow instructions accompanying sprout seed for soaking, rinsing, and storing the product.

 Are heating pads useful for growing microgreens?

Heating pads, also called propagation heat mats, will definitely make microgreen seeds germinate more quickly, something that would be welcome in the case of notoriously slow germinators like celery, lemongrass, and parsley. They are available in easy-to-handle sizes and can be placed under your growing trays and then plugged into an electric outlet. Most quality heat mats on the market today are waterproof and come with thermostats allowing temperature control. Seed that needs a soil temperature of 70 degrees Fahrenheit to germinate, like those just mentioned, could benefit from constant heat delivered directly to the root zone.

That said, I question the need for small-scale home gardeners to invest in expensive heating aids when patience and adherence to proper growing conditions will cause even slowpoke varieties to germinate in good time.

There is a downside to heating pads as well. When they cause plants to dry out from the bottom up, it makes watering much trickier. Better and quicker germination rates and uniform growth patterns in microgreens can be achieved without heat mats or extra kilowatts on the electric bill.

 Q *I have friends who use grow lights to start seeds in their home. Is that something I should consider for microgreens?*

Grow lights should be considered if the place where you live has a paucity of natural light. If it's hard to read the paper in your vintage Victorian manse or city apartment, then check the latest grow-light systems offered at your garden center, in garden catalogs, and online. Grow lights allow you to garden in otherwise-garden-unfriendly spaces, in basements, attics, even closets. Energy-efficient lighting now available makes grow-light systems less expensive to operate, but the initial investment can still run in the hundreds of dollars. Information on do-it-yourself installations, making the upfront costs more affordable, is plentiful online.

A common mistake gardeners make with grow lights is to turn them on in the middle of the night for a few hours rather than extend the time of exposure to light in one continuous sequence. In other words, it is better for your plants if you set a timer on your lights to come on from 3 to 7 am and then again from 5 to 9 pm, in effect lengthening the growing day from 10 hours to 18 hours.

 Q *I've read in some seed catalogs that when plastic domes are fitted over sowing trays, seeds germinate faster and in larger percentages. Should I use domes for my indoor microgreens garden?*

Domes will keep your sowing trays warmer simply by replicating greenhouse conditions for your plants, and that can boost germination rates. But there are a couple of risks associated with using them. In some cases when the gardener's eye and mind are on other things, strong sunlight will pour through the plastic dome and overheat seedlings. Also, domes encourage moisture buildup inside the planted area. Remember, microgreens are sown much closer together than are most outdoor garden crops, so good air circulation is a must for plant health. Domes shut down air movement completely.

Why is cheesecloth a better cover material for my seeds than paper or cloth towels?

Even robust paper towels deteriorate when wet, and after several waterings their sheer weight may compromise seedling growth. Also, paper towels will absorb moisture from the seedbed if you are not vigilant. Linen or other cloth towels are too heavy for tender microgreens and cleaning them after use can be a bother. Horticultural cheesecloth is available to commercial growers but it comes in large rolls way beyond the needs of individual home gardeners. Household cheesecloth found in hardware stores and other retail outlets is suitably porous for crop cover work and can be cut to fit the dimensions of your sowing/growing containers. Make the cloth sturdier by double-layering it.

Is it ever necessary to fertilize microgreen plantings?

For your basic planting medium we recommend an organic soil mix that has some nutritional additives for spurring plant growth, and that is all the sustenance most of your microgreen crops will require. Some microgreens, such as chive, lemongrass, and sorrel, can be sustained through three or more cuttings. These crops will benefit from fertilization following the first harvest. Use fish emulsion, liquid seaweed, or some other mild organic plant food to foster regrowth.

 Q ***Why is it so important to keep everything "organic"?***
Gilbertie's Herb Gardens & Petite Edibles has been certified as an organic grower of herbs, microgreens, and many other plants, following a testing process that is arduous, evidence-based, and complete, so obviously we have a dog in this hunt. However, even without getting into the politics of organic versus chemical, the fact of the matter is that organically grown food crops taste better and are better for your health and for the environment.

Microgreens, which have been termed the new superfood, offer the best example of this because the concentration of flavor and taste in their tiny shoots and seedlings demonstrates that there is a cause-and-effect relationship between the plants and the organic soil mix they are grown in. If you substituted a sterile planting medium or a chemically based soil mix for your organic mix, the microgreens produced would be demonstrably less flavorful and nutritious. Taste-test supermarket lettuces, which always look so big and beautiful in their glistening bin displays, with lettuces grown organically. The latter lettuces may lack luster (excuse the alliteration), but they have more bite and flavor. Scientific studies confirm what lay gardeners have already discovered. Organic farming and gardening practices provide a smarter and safer way of feeding ourselves.

Q *I've read that larger microgreen seeds such as peas and corn benefit from pre-soaking. What are the pros and cons of pre-soaking?*

Peas and corn, and also sunflower and wheatgrass seed, all benefit from being soaked overnight in room-temperature water prior to sowing. These larger seed varieties will not only germinate more quickly after absorbing the moisture, but they will germinate more evenly. This will increase the volume of the crop at harvest, as all shoots will grow to the same desirable height. Before sowing, be sure to drain the seed thoroughly in a colander.

Pre-soaking smaller seed is problematic because it often makes the seed clump together so that sowing evenly across the seedbed becomes an unnecessarily tedious process. That's why I advise against this preliminary step in the case of small seed varieties.

Q *How much of a crop, or successions of crops, does it take to furnish a couple, say, or a family of four, with microgreens throughout the year? We are big salad eaters, so please figure on larger rather than smaller volumes of crops.*

It sounds like you and your family should err on the side of too much production rather than too little. If you figure on a total yield, per 10" x 20" growing tray, of one-third to one-half pound of microgreens, keeping six to eight trays in production (at different stages of growth) should be more than enough to keep you in fresh greens.

A single person living alone, or limited in gardening space, might be able to get by with only two or three trays.

No matter how much or how little you grow, the ready supply of fresh microgreens will bring fresh flavor, color, and texture to your kitchen table.

Q *Should I invest in a pH meter for testing our water and our soil?*

Tools to gauge the degree of acidity or alkalinity in your soil, pH meters can be purchased in garden centers or from garden catalogs for anywhere from under $10 to more than $100. Not surprisingly the costlier meters are likely to produce the most accurate readings.

If you use a commercial organic soil mix for your planting medium, as I suggest, it won't be necessary to do any testing, because the soil mix will have been tested and adjusted to reflect the most beneficial pH for growing plants. If you choose to bring in soil from a garden for growing microgreens, however, it might be a good idea to test that soil first. Send a soil sample to the Cooperative Extension Service (check the U.S. government listings in your phone book for the nearest location). The service is cheap and probably more accurate than any approach you might come up with on your own.

Herb plants and vegetable crops, including microgreens, do best in soil with a pH reading of 6.2 to 6.5. That's the range in which plants are at their most productive, absorbing all the nutrients they need to foster growth.

When the pH registers below that range, it is too sour, or acidic; above, too sweet, or alkaline. Those conditions impede plant growth. Adding lime or potash sweetens soil; adding peat moss or wood chips makes it more acidic.

In the unlikely event that your water supply has an unusually high or low pH, repeated irrigations could affect soil levels.

Q *I've read that microgreens can be added to soups or egg dishes, but do they hold up in the heat?*

Heat and hot water break down the tender, water-based internal structure of microgreens, so any long-term cooking of the greens is not recommended. My rule of thumb when braising or sautéing microgreens is to treat them as you would a tender green like spinach. When adding spinach to an omelet, say, or collards to soup, a brief exposure to heat is all it takes to cook the added ingredient through, without losing its desirable flavor and texture. Incorporate microgreens in your recipes in the same way and you will savor the outcome.

Q *Some gardening authors I've read seem to think it's important to wash microgreens after they have been harvested. Can you give us some guidelines to follow in deciding whether to rinse or not?*

Even though microgreens are grown in a soil base, careful irrigation techniques, such as misting plants with a gentle spray or watering at the bottom of plants, may keep your crops so clean that rinsing will be unnecessary. Also, if you suspend all watering 8–12 hours before harvest, it will help to keep microgreens dry and dirt-free.

If you feel you must rinse microgreens, do so just before putting them to use in recipes and be sure to pat them dry with paper towels. If you want to refrigerate a surplus of harvested microgreens for days at a time, store them unwashed in plastic bags, then take out as needed and rinse and dry just prior to use.

Q *I have two cats. Do I need to protect my crops of microgreens from them?*

First, you certainly don't want a cat treating a sowing tray as its personal litter box! Cheesecloth covers over the seedbeds should discourage such behavior, but it won't hurt to put all pet cats under surveillance for a time, at least at the start of your garden project.

Cats enjoy chewing on catnip, fresh or dried, of course, and also on the wheatgrass that can be grown from seed sold in seed packets under the name "cat grass." I'm not sure cats are attracted to microgreens per se. At least, I haven't heard complaints along that line from cat owners. If you do notice that your cat is showing an inordinate interest in your trays of microgreen plants, one benign deterrent is to give the cat a spray or two from your plant mister. With a few repetitions, that should show the cat who's boss—or not!

Incidentally, among many steps along the way to obtaining certification as an organic grower, Gilbertie's Herb Gardens & Petite Edibles had to agree to follow the federal government's Good Agricultural Practices (GAP) protocol. One of GAP's provisions forbids cats and dogs inside greenhouses. That has meant exiling Ginger, my pet beagle, from the premises. Ginger did not understand the reasons behind this exclusion, and judging by the looks she gives me to this day, she never will.

Q *I live in an area with a long winter. How do the seasons affect microgreen growth rates?*

It happens that most microgreens are cold-weather crops that can be grown in any climate conditions, but the greatly reduced presence of natural light in northern areas, from approximately December 1 to March 1, will slow down growth rates. In a winter climate, with the sun at its shortest daily duration and so far down on the horizon that it generates little warmth, it will take micro-greens one to two weeks longer to reach harvest stage.

The few heat-loving microgreens, such as amaranth and basil, are so slow to germinate and grow in the winter, without the use of heat pads and grow lights, that many gardeners wisely choose to wait until spring to place those crops on their planting schedule.

 I haven't been able to find seed for cucumber microgreens in my catalogs. Are cukes off-limits as a micro?

There are a handful of suppliers for cucumber microgreens, but cucumbers, and squash as well, are not a successful microgreen crop. The problem is, the shoots produced by cucumber seed have virtually no shelf life. In my experience, although they briefly achieve a nutty flavor (but nothing close to fresh cukes), they quickly lose that desirable flavor and texture.

If you want distinctive cucumber flavor in a microgreen, your best bet is to grow the herb salad burnet. It germinates and grows easily and produces leaves with that distinctive cucumber tang.

 Are there microgreens that can be harvested in the wild?

There are a number of edible greens that grow in the wild, though technically most of them are bigger than microgreen size when nature makes them available to us. Foraging for such foods became quite popular after Euell Gibbons published his guidebook *Stalking the Wild Asparagus*, in 1962. Long before Gibbons came on the scene, however, my godmother, Antoinette, was collecting tasty wild greens from the natural landscape. Whenever she came to visit our family in Connecticut from her home in New Jersey during the summer, she brought us a basket of freshly harvested purslane, which grows like a weed—especially in herb and vegetable gardens where it is definitely not welcome. She would gather the prolific grower at stops along the highway. With a flavor comparable to watercress or spinach, purslane (*Portulaca oleracea*) is a welcome addition to salads and other dishes. Quite honestly, as kids we did not always appreciate my godmother's exotic salad course, but my mother was always grateful for her dear friend's contributions.

Dandelion greens *(Taraxacum officinale)* are another popular wild edible, with a pleasing, somewhat bitter taste that also goes well in salads. Lawns that haven't been treated with herbicides are often awash in dandelions. The young greens should be harvested at the peak of their flavor, before those ubiquitous yellow flowers appear. Dandelion greens, by the way, are said to contain greater amounts of vitamins A and K, calcium, and iron than broccoli.

Wood sorrel, which can be found growing in semi-shaded areas in the summer, has been collected and consumed by humans around the world for thousands of years. A member of the large *Oxalis* family, it has an acidic, slightly sour taste similar to that of the cultivated perennial herb sorrel, but the two species are not related botanically.

I single out the three greens mentioned above because they are easy to identify, available for the taking if you know where to look, and they taste good. To locate and harvest most such edibles, you almost have to organize an expeditionary force into the wild. Growing your own microgreens at home is so much easier and just as satisfying.

How accurate are the health benefits claimed for making microgreens a regular part of your diet?

Microgreens came on the culinary scene only recently, and not that much scientific research has been conducted on their nutritional value or their beneficial effects on human health. That said, more than one accredited study has already established that very young, even just days old, vegetable and herb plants contain many times the nutrient value of the fully mature plants they grow into. This biological phenomenon, surprising as it may seem, is what has led some nutritionists and dietitians to declare microgreens a genuine superfood.

Peter Novajosky

 A friend gave me a batch of used seedling trays from a nursery where she worked. How do I prepare them for reuse in growing microgreens?

Rinse all the seedling trays clean with a garden hose, then scrub them in a weak solution of one part household bleach and nine parts water. Rinse again, and they're ready for planting.

Q *I've heard a lot about the dangers of overwatering indoor plants. What should I do to prevent such problems with my microgreens?*

Too much moisture can hurt seeds and seedlings alike. Plants that are slow to develop are especially vulnerable to fungus and mold. Water mold is a dark growth caused by damp conditions. It appears around seedlings and on the soil surface in the spaces between rows. A condition called "damping off" occurs when fungi in the soil attack seeds and seedlings as they begin to develop, killing sprouts as soon as they reach the surface, or after germination, when seedlings reach an inch in height, then wilt and die.

Removing stricken seedlings to a sunnier location and letting them dry out from the top may alleviate the condition. However, if there are fungi present in the soil itself, it is better to discard that soil (not in your healthy garden plot) and start again with fresh, certified organic soil.

Air circulation is almost as important to healthy microgreens as light and warmth. In the winter months, with all the windows in the house shut tight, microgreen greens may stay damp, after watering, for too long. That problem can be avoided by setting up a small portable fan to blow air gently through your plantings.

Good watering techniques will keep your microgreens healthy and fungus-free. Irrigate only when the soil first becomes dry to the touch. Always water (and fertilize, when necessary) at the base of plants, not on top of them, and always in the morning hours.

Peter Novajosky

PART 2

The Recipes

Henry Beary

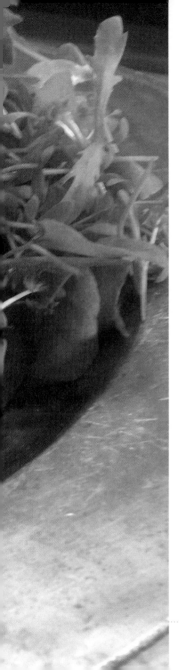

Introduction

I am not a professional chef, and I don't even play one on television, but I love to cook for family and friends. I hope the following selection of recipes will not only show my enthusiasm for serving up delicious healthy fare, but also reveal to you just how versatile fresh microgreens can be in your own meal preparations.

Microgreens add brightness and texture to the simplest recipes for soups and salads, and unexpected flavors to entrées and other dishes. They also make an attractive and highly edible bed for presenting a favorite fish or meat course. I invite you to try some of these recipes in your own kitchen, and also to find inspiration in them by adapting your own recipes with the addition of selected micros.

In most cases our recipes call for the use of specific microgreen varieties, but I am a firm believer in the policy of creative substitution. You may grow only a handful of different micros on your own, and you may not enjoy much of a choice in microgreens in the food markets where you shop—although as their popularity increases these greens are becoming more widely available and in a greater range of choices. Feel free to make substitutions depending on which microgreens are available to you at a given time, and of course according to your personal preferences.

As a guide to creative substitution, take a look at the various blends of herbs and greens that we at Gilbertie's make available to chefs, farmer's markets, and organic food stores. These comprise in effect a palette of flavors, with each family of flavors exhibiting its own qualities in common. Microgreens in the same family may usually be substituted for each other as the need arises without compromising a recipe. This brief summary of our "restaurant blends" organizes the various micro-greens in taste groups that may be useful to you in deciding what micros to use in which recipes:

- Asian offers flavors from the Far East to cool the palate and awaken the taste buds, thanks to pac choi, shungiku, and yukina savoy.
- Citrus is a refreshing mix of the clean flavors and eye-popping colors of ama-ranth, lemon basil, and red-veined sorrel.
- Down to Earth gets its hearty fall flavors from beets, cabbage, Swiss chard, corn shoots, bronze fennel, and mesclun mix.
- Mediterranean, a robust blend with spicy-sweet notes, features arugula, basil, and kale.
- Renee's French is an epicure's collection of beets, purple basil, and chervil, with hints of garlic chive.
- Sal's Mesclun, an eclectic mix of robustly flavored greens, includes arugula, beets, red mustard, red and green Salad Bowl lettuce, and spinach.
- Spicy combines lettuces, mustards, and nasturtiums selected for their pro-nounced stimulation of the senses.
- Tex-Mex captures the zippy flavors of the Southwest with lime basil, garlic chives, and cilantro.

In most of our recipes, microgreen amounts are expressed in cup measures—¼ cup, ½ cup, 1 cup, etc. Generally speaking, a cup of micros equals a single ounce, but that can vary depending on the weight of the microgreen variety. Dill, for example, is super-light compared to relatively heavy radish greens.

Even when microgreens are not integral to a recipe, they can be versatile, hard-working accompaniments to food. Instead of standard-issue lettuces on your sandwiches, use micros; try beet greens for a mild crunch, one of the mustard greens for something spicier, or pea shoots or corn shoots for their garden-fresh flavors.

Soups also invite the use of different microgreen garnishes, depending on the dominant flavor of the soup itself. A tomato-based soup may cry out for Genovese basil or parsley micros as a garnish. For thick soups, try herb croutons or grated cheese blended with a flavorful microgreen. For cream soups, consider chopped, toasted nuts with micros, or a dollop of sour cream or yogurt mixed with fresh garlic chive or cilantro microgreens.

Bon appétit!

Henry Beary

Peter Novajosky

appetizers

Microgreens give a fresh new look and zesty flavor to the small bites I offer guests on the patio or in the den. Two or three micro appetizers are enough for a light supper. Serve pea shoots as stand-alone treats.

Sweet Potato Slices with Micro Pea Shoots

I was astonished to win first prize for this recipe at a recent Saturday-morning farmer's market in Westport, Connecticut. The idea was to see who could do the most with the humble sweet potato, and this appetizer was judged by one of our area's top chefs as the best among the dozen or so entries.

YIELD: 30–36 SLICES

Henry Beary

3 long, narrow sweet potatoes (about 2 lb), peeled and sliced ¼ inch thick

2 Tbsp chopped garlic chive microgreens

2 tsp sea salt

Freshly ground pepper

2 Tbsp (1 oz) unsalted butter, plus 1 Tbsp for the pan

2 cups micro pea shoots, cut 1 to 1½ inches long

2 tsp light olive oil

Preheat the oven to 325 degrees. Butter a large cookie sheet with 1 tablespoon butter and arrange the potato slices on the sheet in a single layer. Sprinkle with the garlic chive microgreens, salt, and pepper to taste. Pinch off small pieces of the remaining 2 tablespoons butter and place a piece on each potato slice. Bake for 20 to 25 minutes.

Place the pea shoots in a small bowl and toss gently with the oil until all the shoots are coated. Place the potato slices on a serving tray and top each slice with 2 or 3 pea shoots—the oil should keep the shoots together and prevent slipping. Serve at room temperature.

Sweet Potato Slices with Microgreens and Crème Fraîche

Here's another sweet potato special that makes excellent finger food. If you can't find crème fraîche, you can use an additional 1 cup of sour cream.

YIELD: 48 SLICES

5 long, narrow sweet potatoes (about 3 lb), peeled and sliced ¼ inch thick

1 tsp sea salt

1 tsp freshly ground white pepper

1 cup crème fraîche

½ cup sour cream

½ cup equal parts amaranth, radish, and red-veined sorrel microgreens

Cover the potato slices with cold water and let soak for 15 minutes. Bring a large pot of fresh water to a boil; add the potatoes, salt, and pepper. Reduce the heat and simmer until the potatoes are tender but still firm, about 5 minutes.

Drain the potatoes and dry on paper towels; transfer to a serving tray. In a small bowl, combine the crème fraîche and sour cream. Place 1 teaspoon of the cream mixture on each potato slice and garnish with the microgreens. Refrigerate for up to 1 hour before serving.

Sautéed Cherry Tomatoes with Micros

Small cherry tomatoes work best in this recipe, which also can be used as a side dish to accompany an entrée.

YIELD: 8–10 SERVINGS

2 Tbsp extra-virgin olive oil

2 pints small cherry tomatoes

1 cup equal parts celery, cress, and parsley
    microgreens

1 tsp fresh lemon juice

½ tsp sea salt

Freshly ground pepper

Toast points or crackers

Heat the oil in a large skillet over medium heat, add the tomatoes, and cook for 2 to 3 minutes, stirring constantly to coat the tomatoes evenly. Add the microgreens, lemon juice, salt, and pepper to taste and continue to cook, stirring, for 1 minute. Serve hot on toast points or crackers.

Henry Beary

Shrimp Grilled in Fresh Basil Leaves

This is a fabulous accompaniment to summer cocktails on the porch or terrace; the crunchy bed of microgreens adds a salad element.

YIELD: 6 SERVINGS

24 large shrimp, peeled and deveined, tails left
   intact
4 Tbsp (2 oz) unsalted butter, melted
3 Tbsp fresh lime juice
½ tsp red pepper flakes
24 large basil leaves, about 2 inches long, rinsed
   and patted dry
12 bamboo skewers, soaked in water for 30 minutes
½ cup equal parts lemon basil and fennel
   microgreens

Preheat a grill to high heat. In a large bowl, toss the shrimp with the melted butter, lime juice, and pepper flakes. Fold a basil leaf around each shrimp. Thread 2 wrapped shrimp on each skewer and brush with any remaining butter mixture. Grill, turning once, for 4 minutes. Arrange the microgreens on a platter, set the shrimp skewers on the microgreens, and serve.

Henry Beary

Smoked Salmon with Radish and Salad Burnet Microgreens

The micros add tang and texture to this classic salmon hors d'oeuvre.

YIELD: 4–8 SERVINGS

8 oz cream cheese, softened

1 Tbsp lemon juice

Dash freshly ground pepper

¼ cup chopped salad burnet microgreens

¼ cup chopped radish microgreens

6 oz smoked salmon, chopped

2 Tbsp (1 oz) unsalted butter, melted

Thinly sliced rye bread

Oil a 2- to 3-cup mold and set aside. In a medium bowl, stir together the cream cheese, lemon juice, and pepper until smooth. Stir in the microgreens, smoked salmon, and melted butter. Pack into the mold and refrigerate until firm, about 4 hours. Unmold onto a serving platter and surround with rye bread slices; serve.

soups

Almost all soups, hot or cold, look more inviting when garnished with fresh micros, and they develop more intriguing flavors when one or more of the tangier microgreens are worked into recipes. When possible, make soups from your own homemade stock to add richness and depth. When using store-bought stock or broth, look for low-salt organic brands.

Chilled Microgreens Soup

Here's a soup filled with the bright flavors of fresh microgreens. Serve with crusty bread and home-made iced tea for an elegant summer lunch.

YIELD: 8 SERVINGS

2 Tbsp (1 oz) unsalted butter

2 tsp canola oil

1 lb sweet onions (such as Vidalia or Walla Walla), chopped

¼ cup all-purpose flour

4 cups vegetable stock or broth

1 cup dry white wine

2 cups parsley microgreens

1 cup garlic chive microgreens

¼ cup salad burnet microgreens

⅔ cup low-fat or nonfat sour cream, plus extra for serving

1 tsp sea salt

¼ tsp freshly ground pepper

1 tsp herb vinegar or lemon juice

Minced fresh herbs or edible flowers

In a large saucepan, heat the butter and oil over medium heat. Add the onions and cook, stirring occasionally, for about 8 minutes, or until the onions are soft. Sprinkle the flour over the onions and cook, stirring, for 3 minutes. Stir in the stock and wine and cook, stirring, for 2 minutes, or until slightly thickened. Remove from the heat and stir in the microgreens. Cool to lukewarm.

Working in batches, process the soup in a blender until very smooth. Transfer to a container and whisk in the sour cream, salt, and pepper. Cover and refrigerate for at least 4 hours but not more than 24 hours. Just before serving, stir in the vinegar. Garnish with dollops of sour cream, sprinkle with herbs, and serve.

Micro Lovage and Basil Soup

Lovage enhances this quick, easily made soup, giving it an undertone of celery flavor and an attractive pale green color. Increase the tanginess by using lemon basil or augment the sweet-spicy aroma by mixing in some cinnamon basil. Garnish with micro basil leaves.

YIELD: 4–6 SERVINGS

2 Tbsp (1 oz) unsalted butter

1 Tbsp canola oil

2 medium yellow onions, chopped (2 cups)

8 oz potatoes, peeled and cut into ½-inch pieces

½ cup lovage microgreens

2 cups vegetable stock or broth

½ cup dry white wine

½ cup water

1 cup fresh basil leaves (cinnamon, Genovese, or lemon)

In a large saucepan, heat the butter and oil over medium-high heat. Add the onions and cook, stirring, for about 6 minutes, or until soft. Add the potatoes and microgreens and cook, stirring, for about 5 minutes or until the potatoes lose their raw look. Stir in the stock, wine, and water. Cover, reduce the heat to low, and simmer about 30 minutes, or until the potatoes are very tender. Add the basil and cook for 30 seconds. Remove from the heat and process in a blender, food processor, or food mill until smooth. Serve immediately or refrigerate and serve cold.

Microgreen Borscht

This is a light version of borscht, a cooling way to begin a family meal or light summer luncheon. It's a snap to throw together and can be served cold with a dollop of sour cream or hot as a dressy first course.

YIELD: 4–6 SERVINGS

1 lb beets, peeled and grated

¼ cup red wine vinegar

4 cups chicken stock or broth

2 medium carrots, peeled and sliced

½ cup garlic chive microgreens

4 cups kale microgreens

Sea salt and freshly ground pepper

Sour cream

Dill microgreen sprigs

Combine ½ cup of the grated beets with the vinegar; set aside to soak. In a large saucepan, combine the stock, carrots, and garlic chive microgreens, bring to a simmer, and cook for 10 minutes. Add the remaining beets and cook until tender, about 15 minutes. Add the kale microgreens and cook for 3 minutes. Add the reserved vinegar and beets and season with salt and pepper to taste. Serve hot, warm, or chilled with a dollop of sour cream and sprigs of dill microgreens.

Henry Beary

Mighty Micro Beta Soup

This soup, as good for you as it is delicious, makes the most of the beta-carotene and antioxidants found in fresh microgreens.

YIELD: 6 SERVINGS

1 Tbsp canola oil or extra-virgin olive oil

1 medium yellow onion, diced (1 cup)

¼ cup chopped lovage microgreens

2 garlic cloves, minced

1½ cups thinly sliced carrots

1 cup diced sweet potatoes

1 cup diced winter squash

1 cup peeled, seeded, and chopped tomatoes

4 cups vegetable stock or broth

½ cup dry white wine

8 oz green beans, cut into 1-inch lengths, or 1 (10-oz) package frozen green beans, thawed

2 cups equal parts kale, spinach, and Swiss chard microgreens

1 cup spinach rotelle or elbow pasta

In a large saucepan, heat the oil over medium heat. Add the onion and cook, stirring occasionally, for 3 to 5 minutes, or until soft. Add the lovage microgreens and garlic and cook for 1 to 2 minutes. Add the carrots, sweet potatoes, squash, tomatoes, stock, and wine and bring to a simmer, stirring occasionally. Reduce the heat to low, cover, and cook for 30 minutes, or until the vegetables are tender. Add the green beans; kale, spinach, and Swiss chard microgreens; and pasta. Increase the heat to medium and cook for 15 minutes, or until the pasta is done. Serve immediately.

Sorrel Vichyssoise

The classic French soup gets a microgreen update.

YIELD: 6 SERVINGS

2 Tbsp (1 oz) unsalted butter

2 Tbsp canola oil

2 medium yellow onions, chopped (2 cups)

3 leeks, white parts only, washed thoroughly and cut into 1-inch sections (4 cups)

1 lb potatoes, peeled and cut into ½-inch pieces

1 bay leaf

4 cups vegetable stock or broth

1 cup sorrel microgreens

½ cup heavy cream

½ cup milk

½ tsp ground mace or nutmeg

½ tsp freshly ground white pepper

Garlic chive and scallion microgreens

In a large saucepan, heat the butter and oil over medium heat. Add the onions and leeks and cook, stirring frequently, for about 8 minutes or until soft. Add the potatoes and bay leaf and cook for another 3 minutes, continuing to stir. Add the stock, bring to a simmer, then reduce the heat to low, cover, and cook about 20 minutes, or until the potatoes are very tender.

Remove the bay leaf. Stir in the sorrel microgreens, cream, milk, and mace and cook just until hot. Remove from the heat and, working in batches, process the soup in a blender or food processor until smooth. Stir in the white pepper. Serve immediately or refrigerate and serve cold, garnished with garlic chive and scallion microgreens.

Henry Beary

Mediterranean Garden Soup

When your vegetable garden or the nearest farm stand is brimming with red, ripe tomatoes, yellow and green zucchini, deep purple eggplant, and fat leeks, a bowl of this family-style soup, spiced up with fresh microgreens, will hit the spot. Pamper your guests by serving this soup in bowls that have been warmed in a 200-degree oven for 2 to 3 minutes.

YIELD: 6–8 SERVINGS

8 cups chicken stock or broth

1 cup dry white wine

¼ cup dried small white beans, soaked in water for 2 hours and drained

3 small red-skinned potatoes, cut into 1-inch dice.

1 large onion, cut into 1-inch dice

2 leeks, trimmed, cut into thin 2-inch-long strips and rinsed thoroughly

2 carrots, cut into thin 2-inch-long strips

3 celery stalks, cut into thin 2-inch-long strips

1 medium eggplant, cut into 1-inch dice

1 zucchini, cut into 1-inch dice

1 yellow crookneck squash, cut into 1-inch dice

2 large ripe tomatoes, peeled, seeded, and chopped

½ cup chopped garlic chive microgreens

½ cup basil microgreens

1 cup parsley microgreens

Sea salt and freshly ground pepper

In a large soup pot, bring the stock and wine to a boil. Reduce the heat, add the beans, and simmer for 15 minutes. Add the potatoes, onion, leeks, carrots, and celery and simmer for 15 minutes. Add the eggplant, zucchini, yellow squash, tomatoes, and microgreens and continue to simmer until all the vegetable are tender. Season with salt and pepper to taste. Ladle into heated soup bowls and serve.

Gazpacho à la Micro

Serve this cooling soup in chilled clear glass mugs for a summery first course while herb-wrapped steaks and garden vegetables are grilling. The dazzling combination of the fruit and vegetable flavors is heightened by the fresh cilantro.

YIELD: 4 SERVINGS

1 medium cantaloupe, peeled, seeded, and finely chopped

2 large ripe tomatoes, peeled, seeded, and finely chopped

1 yellow bell pepper, stemmed, seeded, and chopped

1 red bell pepper, stemmed, seeded, and chopped

1 large onion, chopped

2 jalapeño chiles, stemmed, seeded, and minced

¼ cup chopped garlic chive microgreens

¼ cup chopped cilantro microgreens, plus cilantro microgreen sprigs for garnish

Grated zest of 1 orange, plus 1½ cups fresh orange juice (3 oranges)

Grated zest of 1 lime, plus 3 Tbsp fresh lime juice (2 limes)

Sea salt and freshly ground pepper

In a large bowl, combine the cantaloupe, tomatoes, bell peppers, onion, jalapeños, and chopped microgreens. Add the orange zest and juice and lime zest and juice and stir. Season with salt and pepper to taste. Cover and refrigerate for at least 1 hour. Ladle into chilled soup bowls, garnish with sprigs of cilantro microgreens, and serve.

Chilled Zucchini Soup with Spicy Microgreens

A rich, smooth version of a popular summer chilled soup, the recipe can be made with a coarser texture, if desired, simply by omitting the sieve stage in the directions.

YIELD: 6–8 SERVINGS

¼ cup extra-virgin olive oil
6–8 medium zucchini, diced
½ cup garlic chive microgreens
½ cup cress microgreens
½ cup mustard microgreens
4 cups crème fraîche or heavy cream
Sea salt and freshly ground pepper

In a large, heavy saucepan, heat the oil over medium heat. Add the zucchini; reduce the heat to low and cook, covered for, 10 to 15 minutes or until the zucchini are very tender but not browned. Cool slightly and stir in 2 cups of the crème fraîche and the microgreens.

Working in batches, process the soup in a blender or food processor until smooth. Stir in the remaining crème fraîche, season with salt and pepper to taste, cover, and refrigerate for at least 1 hour before serving.

Henry Beary

salads

Handfuls of three or more microgreens, mixed together and tossed with a simple vinaigrette or other dressing, stand on their own as a light salad for lunch or dinner. Or power up an ordinary garden salad with the addition of crunchy micros such as pea shoots, pac choi, or garlic chives.

Chopped Salad with Mesclun Microgreens

This salad takes full advantage of the bounty of the end-of-summer farm stand.

YIELD: 4 SERVINGS

2 large red bell peppers, stemmed, seeded, and chopped

2 large tomatoes, peeled and coarsely chopped

3 small zucchini, coarsely chopped

5 Tbsp white wine vinegar

½ tsp sea salt

¾ cup extra-virgin olive oil

2 cups mesclun salad microgreens

1 small Vidalia, Walla Walla, or Spanish onion, thinly sliced

¼ cup crumbled feta cheese

In a large bowl, toss together the bell peppers, tomatoes, and zucchini. Process the vinegar and salt in a blender or food processor to blend. While the machine is running, slowly add the oil and process until smooth. Pour the dressing over the vegetables and toss to coat. Line four plates with the microgreens. Mound the vegetables onto the greens and top with the sliced onion and feta cheese. Serve.

Mint Microgreen Chopped Salad

This refreshing chopped salad variation gets a lift from the perky combination of fresh mint, citrusy micros, and feta cheese.

YIELD: 4 SERVINGS

2 large red bell peppers, stemmed, seeded, and chopped

2 large tomatoes, peeled and coarsely chopped

3 small zucchini, coarsely chopped

1 cup chopped spearmint leaves

5 Tbsp white wine vinegar

½ tsp sea salt

¾ cup extra-virgin olive oil

½ cup equal parts chopped lemon basil, celery, and chervil microgreens,

1 small Vidalia, Walla Walla, or Spanish onion, thinly sliced

¼ cup crumbled feta cheese

In a large bowl, toss together the bell peppers, tomatoes, and zucchini. Process the mint, vinegar, and salt in a blender or food processor to blend. While the machine is running, slowly add the oil and process until smooth. Pour the dressing over the vegetables and toss to coat. Line four plates with the microgreens. Mound the vegetables onto the greens and top with the sliced onion and feta cheese. Serve.

Salad Greens in Walnut Sauce

This is a nice, chunky, and nutty change-of-pace salad for a fall or winter menu.

YIELD: 2–3 SERVINGS

¾ cup chopped walnuts

¼ cup grated Parmesan cheese

3 Tbsp extra-virgin olive oil

1 garlic clove, finely minced

Sea salt and freshly ground pepper

2 cups equal parts chopped arugula, lime basil, and kale microgreens

In a large bowl, combine the walnuts, Parmesan, oil, and garlic and season with salt and pepper to taste. Add the microgreens, mix well, and serve.

Henry Beary

Sweet Potato Salad with Pea Shoots

Here's a colorful salad definitely worth the fuss—everyone loves that crisp, fresh-as-spring Jack-and-the-Pea-Stalk taste of pea micros.

YIELD: 6 SERVINGS

1¼ lb sweet potatoes, peeled

1 lb haricots verts (or tender young green beans)

1 large onion, halved and thinly sliced

½ cup dry white wine

2 garlic cloves, minced

¼ cup crème fraîche

2 Tbsp extra-virgin olive oil

1 Tbsp Dijon mustard

½ cup chopped pea shoot microgreens

Place the potatoes in a large saucepan of cold, salted water. Bring to a boil and cook until tender but still firm. Drain the potatoes, cool, and slice into ¼-inch slices. Transfer to a large bowl. Fit a second large saucepan with a steamer basket, add 1 inch of water, and bring to a rapid boil. Add the haricots verts, cover, and steam until just tender. Transfer the haricots verts to the bowl with the potatoes, add the onion, and toss gently.

For the dressing, bring the white wine to a boil in a small saucepan. Reduce the heat, add the garlic, and simmer for 5 minutes. Remove from the heat and whisk in the crème fraîche, oil, mustard, and microgreens. Pour the dressing over the vegetables, toss to coat, and serve.

Green Bean Salad

Simple to prepare, even easier to enjoy. The dressing itself can be used on salads and other vegetable dishes if desired.

YIELD: 6 SERVINGS

1 lb green beans, trimmed
¼ cup sour cream
1 shallot, peeled
1 Tbsp extra-virgin olive oil
1 Tbsp balsamic vinegar
1 garlic clove, peeled
1 tsp Dijon mustard
½ cup equal parts chopped arugula, cress, and
   shungiku microgreens
Sea salt and freshly ground pepper

Bring a medium saucepan of salted water to a boil, add the green beans, and cook until just tender, about 3 minutes. Drain and rinse under running cold water; shake dry and transfer to a large bowl. Process the sour cream, shallot, oil, vinegar, garlic, and mustard in a blender or food processor until smooth. Season with salt and pepper to taste. Pour the dressing over the beans, add the microgreens, and toss to coat evenly. Cover and refrigerate for 2 hours before serving.

Henry Beary

Warm Eggplant Salad with Amaranth, Basil, and Sorrel Microgreens

Thanks to microgreens, this recipe brings an earthy flavor dimension to an unusual eggplant dish.

YIELD: 4 SERVINGS

2 large tomatoes, peeled, seeded, and chopped

4 shallots, minced

¼ cup extra-virgin olive oil, plus extra for brushing the eggplants

3 Tbsp white wine vinegar

Sea salt and freshly ground pepper

2 small white eggplants

2 small purple eggplants

¼ cup equal parts chopped amaranth, basil, and sorrel microgreens

In a large bowl, combine the tomatoes and shallots. Add the oil and vinegar and season with salt and pepper to taste. Refrigerate for 30 minutes to combine the flavors. Place four salad plates in the refrigerator to chill.

Meanwhile, preheat a grill to low heat. Cut the eggplants into thin slices lengthwise. Sprinkle with salt and pepper to taste; brush both sides with additional oil. Grill the eggplant until browned on both sides, brushing with oil as needed to keep moistened. Remove from the grill and cover to keep warm.

Divide the tomato-shallot mixture among the chilled plates. Arrange the eggplant slices over the tomatoes, sprinkle the microgreens over the eggplant, and serve.

Sylvan Salad Bowl

This pear salad with strong tarragon overtones is perfect for a brunch menu. It was originally created by Frances Towner Giedt, a food writer from Texas who helped me with my book Herbs for the Holidays. The recipe gets its name from the street location of our retail garden center in Westport, Connecticut. We've been there ninety-two years!

YIELD: 6 SERVINGS

½ cup equal parts beet, cress, and kale microgreens
4 oz goat cheese
3 medium red or white Bartlett pears, halved and cored
1 Tbsp fresh lemon juice
½ cup extra-virgin olive oil
3 Tbsp tarragon vinegar
1 Tbsp chopped tarragon microgreens
1 Tbsp minced red onion
Freshly ground pepper

Divide the beet, cress, and kale microgreens evenly among six salad plates. Slice the goat cheese into six pieces and place one piece on each plate. Cut the pear halves into wedges and brush the cut surfaces with the lemon juice. Arrange a few pear slices around each piece of cheese. In a small bowl, beat together the oil, vinegar, tarragon microgreens, and red onion. Drizzle each salad with dressing and sprinkle with pepper to taste. Serve.

Henry Beary

Henry Beary

Couscous Salad with Beet, Chard, Fennel, and Mesclun Microgreens

Please note: This salad tastes best after an overnight rest to meld the flavors, so plan accordingly. This elaborate concoction will put you on a flying carpet to the exotic tastes and fragrances of North Africa and the Near East. Don't forget your fez!

YIELD: 4–6 SERVINGS

2 cups chicken stock or broth

3 Tbsp extra-virgin olive oil

1 tsp ground cumin

1 tsp ground ginger

Dash ground cinnamon

1 cup pearl couscous

¼ cup dried currants

¼ cup chopped pitted dates

1 cup diced zucchini

½ cup diced carrots

½ cup diced red onion

2 Tbsp fresh lemon juice

Sea salt and freshly ground pepper

¼ cup pine nuts

1 cup equal parts beet, chard, fennel, and mesclun microgreens

In a medium saucepan, bring the stock, 2 tablespoons of the oil, the cumin, ginger, and cinnamon to a boil. Stir in the couscous and cook until most of the liquid is absorbed, about 2 minutes. Remove from the heat and stir in the currants and dates. Cover tightly and let stand for 15 minutes. Add the zucchini, carrots, and onion.

In a small bowl, combine the lemon juice and remaining 1 tablespoon oil. Pour over the couscous; toss to coat thoroughly. Refrigerate overnight to blend the flavors. Bring to room temperature, toss with the pine nuts and microgreens, and serve.

Henry Beary

entrées

Grilled, baked, or broiled, meat and fish courses emerge with surprisingly savory flavors when dressed with microgreens or bathed in a micro marinade.

Orange–Lemon Basil Beef Kabobs

It takes a little time to thread the skewers properly, but they look great on the grill and taste even better.

YIELD: 4 SERVINGS

½ cup fresh orange juice, plus 2 medium thin-
skinned oranges, unpeeled
¼ cup chopped garlic chive microgreens
¼ cup chopped lemon basil microgreens
3 Tbsp extra-virgin olive oil
1½ lb lean boneless sirloin, trimmed
4 bamboo skewers, soaked in water for 30 minutes

In a medium bowl, combine the orange juice, micro-greens, and oil. Slice the steak diagonally across the grain into ¼-inch-wide strips, add to the juice mixture and stir to coat. Marinate the steak for 30 minutes.

While the steak marinates, preheat a grill to medium-high heat. Slice the oranges crosswise into ½-inch slices; cut each slice into 8 wedges. Weave the steak onto the skewers accordion-style, placing an orange wedge between each loop. Grill the skewered beef, turning and basting with the marinade, for 5 to 10 minutes. (Stop basting a minute or two before the meat is done.) Serve immediately.

Grilled Veal Chops Jalisco

The spicy flavors of Old Mexico permeate this grill special.

YIELD: 4 SERVINGS

3 cups fresh orange juice (6 oranges)
¼ cup chopped garlic chive microgreens
¼ cup chopped mustard green microgreens
½ cup chopped cilantro microgreens
1 small jalapeño chile, seeded and chopped
4 veal chops, 1½ inches thick, trimmed

In a medium bowl, combine the orange juice, microgreens, and jalapeño. Place the chops in a large, shallow dish, pour the juice mixture over the chops, cover, and refrigerate for 2 hours, turning occasionally.

While the chops marinate, preheat a grill to medium heat. Grill the chops 5 minutes per side for medium-rare, brushing frequently with the marinade. (Stop basting a few minutes before the chops are done.) Serve.

Steamed Fish with Ginger and Red Chile Peppers

Asian flavors add a kick to the fish, leavened by the earthy goodness of fresh basil, beet, and chervil microgreens.

YIELD: 4 SERVINGS

2 oz Chinese fermented black beans, rinsed and drained thoroughly

2 small fresh red chile peppers, seeded and finely chopped

3 scallions, minced

1 Tbsp minced fresh ginger

1 garlic clove, minced

1 (1½- to 2-lb) whole fish, such as red snapper or sea bass, cleaned and patted dry

2 Tbsp dry white wine

1 Tbsp peanut oil

1 Tbsp soy sauce

3 sprigs fresh cilantro

1 cup equal parts chopped basil, beet, and chervil microgreens

Coarsely chop the beans and combine them with the chiles, scallions, ginger, and garlic. Place the fish on a steaming rack in a roasting pan to which a cup of water has been added. Position the pan over a large burner on your stovetop. Spread the bean mixture over the fish. Sprinkle with the wine; drizzle with the oil and soy sauce. Lay the cilantro sprigs on the fish and cover the pan. Steam, covered, over medium heat for 15 to 20 minutes, or until the fish flakes easily. Transfer the fish to a heated serving platter. Sprinkle with the chopped microgreens and serve.

Henry Beary

Grilled Pork Tenderloins Seasoned with Micros

The microgreen-based marinade gives the pork a fresh, spicy flavor while preserving its moistness.

YIELD: 4 SERVINGS

2 (12-oz) pork tenderloins, trimmed
½ cup raspberry vinegar
¼ cup chopped garlic chive microgreens
¼ cup chopped cilantro microgreens
1 Tbsp honey
1 tsp Dijon mustard
¼ tsp freshly ground pepper
1 cup arugula microgreens

Place the tenderloins in a shallow baking dish. In a small bowl, whisk together the vinegar, garlic chive microgreens, cilantro microgreens, honey, mustard, and pepper. Pour over the pork, cover, and refrigerate for 2 hours, turning occasionally.

While the tenderloins marinate, preheat a grill to medium heat. Grill the tenderloins for 20 to 30 minutes, basting frequently with the marinade. (Stop basting a minute or two before the tenderloins are done.) Remove from the heat, slice thinly across the grain, and serve on a bed of arugula microgreens.

Chicken Paillards with Vinegar Sauce and Easy-as-ABC Micros

Arugula, beet, and chervil microgreens are the ABC building blocks of the salad bed underlying this tart-sweet chicken favorite.

YIELD: 6 SERVINGS

6 boneless, skinless chicken breasts, trimmed

½ cup extra-virgin olive oil

1 Tbsp minced fresh thyme

1 Tbsp minced parsley

1 garlic clove, minced

1 bay leaf

2 whole cloves

4 cups chicken stock or broth

2 Granny Smith apples, cored and sliced

2 Tbsp cider vinegar

Sea salt and freshly ground pepper

4 cups arugula, beet, and chervil microgreens

Place the chicken breasts between two pieces of wax paper and pound with a mallet until very thin. Combine ¼ cup of the oil, the thyme, parsley, garlic, bay leaf and whole cloves in a shallow dish large enough to hold the chicken breasts in one layer.

Add the chicken to the oil-herb mixture, turning once to coat well. Cover and refrigerate for 3 hours.

Meanwhile, in a large saucepan, bring the stock to a boil. Add the apples and vinegar and simmer for 30 minutes, until the apples are very tender. Remove the apples from the stock and process them in a food processor or blender until smooth. Return the apple purée to the saucepan and continue to cook over low heat until thick. Season with salt and pepper to taste. Keep warm.

Preheat a grill to medium heat or preheat the broiler. Grill or broil the chicken, about 1 minute per side. Cut the chicken breasts into thick slices.

Toss the microgreens with the remaining ¼ cup oil and season with salt and pepper to taste. Divide the microgreens among six plates. Arrange the chicken slices over the microgreens and spoon the sauce over the chicken. Serve.

Asian Microgreen Chicken Tenders

*Here's a spicy fast-track supper even the kids will
enjoy. Serve over rice.*

YIELD: 4 SERVINGS

¼ cup soy sauce

¼ cup dry sherry

1 Tbsp chopped fresh ginger

2 garlic cloves, minced

2 tsp cornstarch

½ tsp red pepper flakes

1 lb boneless, skinless chicken breasts, trimmed and
   cut into 1-inch-wide strips

1 cup equal parts pac choi, shungiku, and yukina
   savoy microgreens

½ cup fresh basil microgreens

3 Tbsp vegetable oil

1 large onion, halved and thinly sliced

In a medium bowl, whisk together the soy sauce,
sherry, ginger, garlic, cornstarch, and pepper flakes.
Add the chicken, half of the Asian microgreens, and
the basil microgreens, and stir to coat. Marinate for
30 minutes.

Heat 2 tablespoons of the oil in a large skillet or
wok. With a slotted spoon, transfer the chicken
to the skillet, reserving the marinade. Stir-fry for 4
minutes. Add the remaining oil, the onion, and the
remaining Asian microgreens. Stir-fry for 2 minutes.
Add the reserved marinade and cook for 1 to 2
minutes, until thickened. Serve.

Grilled Chicken in Microgreen Marinade

Coated with dense flavor and moist to the core, these chicken breasts will make for a memorable Sunday supper.

YIELD: 4 SERVINGS

¾ cup equal parts basil, cress, and radish microgreens
1 Tbsp grated Parmesan cheese
1 Tbsp pine nuts, toasted
1 garlic clove, cut in half
¼ cup plain yogurt
4 boneless, skinless chicken breasts, trimmed
½ cup arugula microgreens

Process half of the basil, cress, and radish microgreens; the Parmesan; pine nuts; and garlic in a food processor until smooth. Add the yogurt and process briefly to blend. Place the chicken in a shallow dish and cover with the microgreen mixture, turning to coat all sides. Cover and refrigerate for 2 hours.

While the chicken marinates, preheat a grill to medium-high heat. Grill the chicken, basting occasionally with the marinade, until tender, about 5 minutes per side. (Stop basting a minute or two before the chicken is done.) Divide the arugula microgreens and remaining basil, cress, and radish microgreens evenly among four plates, place a chicken breast on each plate, and serve.

Henry Beary

Keller Farm Lamb Chops

The Keller family farm in Easton, Connecticut, was the original occupant of the land we purchased in 1984 for our greenhouses. The farm was noted for its milk cows and grass-fed lamb. A piquant marinade brings out the best in these low-fat, high-flavor chops.

YIELD: 6 SERVINGS

6 (5- to 6-oz) lamb loin chops, 2 inches thick, trimmed
⅓ cup extra-virgin olive oil
3 Tbsp chopped mustard microgreens
2 Tbsp chopped fresh basil
2 garlic cloves, minced
3 Tbsp dry white wine
1 Tbsp white wine vinegar
1 cup equal parts cress and sorrel microgreens

Combine the oil, mustard microgreens, basil, garlic, wine, and vinegar. Place the chops in marinade, turning to coat both sides. Let stand at room temperature for 30 minutes, turning often.

While the lamb chops marinate, preheat a grill to medium-high heat or preheat the broiler. Grill or broil the chops for 7 to 8 minutes per side, or to the desired doneness, brushing with the remaining marinade. (Stop basting a minute or two before the chops are done.) Serve over the cress and sorrel microgreens.

Salmon Molyneaux

We made friends with Earl and Lorraine Molyneaux, who owned and operated Salmon River Lodge in Kimberly, Idaho, one summer when I took two of my children, Celeste and Tom, out West on a trail-riding adventure. This recipe was served to us one night with fish caught on the fly in the Salmon River earlier in the day.

YIELD: 4 SERVINGS

1 cup chicken stock or broth

1 cup dry white wine

½ cup water

¼ cup chopped fennel microgreens

¼ cup chopped dill microgreens

1 small onion, finely chopped

4 (5- to 6-oz) skin-on salmon fillets, 1 inch thick

Sea salt and freshly ground pepper

½ cup heavy cream

In a large skillet, bring the broth to a boil. Add the wine, water, microgreens, and onion. Season the salmon with salt and pepper to taste and add it to the skillet. Cover, reduce the heat, and simmer for 10 minutes, until the fish flakes easily. Remove the salmon; keep warm. Over high heat, reduce the liquid to ½ cup. Stir in the cream and cook until thickened. Arrange the salmon on serving plates, top with the sauce, and serve.

Broiled Salmon in Lemon, Mizuna, and Saltwort Sauce

This classic marriage of Asian flavors brings out the best in fresh-caught salmon.

YIELD: 10–12 SERVINGS

Juice from 2 lemons
8 shallots, minced
¼ cup mizuna microgreens
¼ cup saltwort microgreens
1 (3-lb) salmon fillet, skin-on
¼ cup extra-virgin olive oil
Freshly ground pepper

Preheat the oven to 350°F. Mix the lemon juice and microgreens in a broiler pan or a broiler-proof baking pan. Add the salmon fillet and turn several times until fully covered with the microgreen mixture. Turn the salmon skin side down, pour the oil over the top, and sprinkle with pepper. Bake for about 5 minutes. Remove from the oven and baste heavily with pan juices. (Do not turn the fillet.) Heat the oven broiler and broil the salmon on an upper rack for 5 minutes. Serve.

Grilled Salmon Flavored with Lemon Basil, Beet, and Sorrel

Rubbed with this microgreen combo, salmon responds in subtle and savory ways.

YIELD: 6–8 SERVINGS

1 (3- to 4-lb) salmon fillet

¼ cup fresh lemon juice (2 lemons)

2 Tbsp extra-virgin olive oil

2 scallions, thinly sliced

⅛ tsp freshly ground pepper

½ cup equal parts chopped lemon basil, beet, and sorrel microgreens

Preheat a grill to medium-high heat. Place the salmon on a sheet of heavy-duty foil, trimming the foil to fit under the fillet. Combine the microgreens, scallions, lemon juice, oil, and pepper in a small bowl. Place the salmon, still on the foil, on the grill, 5 to 6 inches from the heat source, and baste with the microgreen mixture. Grill, without turning, until the salmon is done, about 20 minutes, basting frequently. (Stop basting a minute or two before the salmon is done.) Serve.

Henry Beary

Grilled Tuna with Asian Microgreen Sauce

This versatile sauce, with its savory microgreen overtones, perfectly complements the tuna, but it's equally great spooned over other grilled or broiled fish or chicken. You can also use it to add some bite to steamed vegetables.

YIELD: 4 SERVINGS

1 cup equal parts chopped pac choi, shungiku, and yukina savoy microgreens
1 large tomato, peeled, seeded, and chopped
½ cup chopped green bell pepper
¼ cup chopped scallions
2 Tbsp chopped canned green chiles
1 Tbsp fresh lemon juice
4 (6-oz) tuna fillets or steaks, 1 inch thick
Extra-virgin olive oil
Sea salt and freshly ground pepper

Preheat a grill to high heat or preheat a broiler. In a medium bowl, combine the microgreens, tomato, pepper, green onion, chiles, and lemon juice; set aside. Rub the tuna with oil and season with salt and pepper. Grill or broil the tuna, turning once or twice, for 5 minutes. Spoon the sauce over the tuna and serve.

Country Microgreen Omelet

Although more commonly a brunch item than an entrée, omelets are the perfect medium for micro-greens, as they are for various herbs and greens such as spinach. Let the home chef be the taste-maker, choosing the micros that deliver mild, spicy, earthy, or a combination of all those flavors.

YIELD: 4 SERVINGS

2 Tbsp (1 oz) unsalted butter

¼ cup chopped green bell pepper

5 eggs, lightly beaten

½ cup equal parts chopped mustard, radish, and
    watercress microgreens

¼ cup shredded Monterey Jack cheese

¼ cup chopped tomatoes

1 Tbsp chopped fresh cilantro

¼ cup sour cream

2 slices bacon, fried until crisp

Sea salt and freshly ground pepper

Melt the butter in a large skillet over medium-high heat. Add the bell pepper and cook, stirring, for 3 minutes. Pour the eggs into the skillet and cook, lifting from the bottom and allowing the uncooked portion to flow underneath. When the eggs are almost set, sprinkle evenly with the microgreens, cheese, tomatoes, and cilantro. Cover and heat just until the cheese melts. Remove from the heat and mound the sour cream in the center. Crumble the bacon over the omelet, season with salt and pepper to taste, and serve.

Note: For an omelet with a lighter consistency, stir 5 tablespoons of water into the eggs before cooking.

Henry Beary

Peter Novajosky

side dishes

*Spicy microgreens like mustard and cress and colorful micros
like purple amaranth, red basil, and yellow corn shoots
can make the difference between a bland vegetable dish
and one that rocks the table.*

Sliced Potatoes and Turnips with Microgreens

Ordinary root vegetables are given an uncommonly savory tang in this easy-to-make side dish.

YIELD: 4 SERVINGS

5 medium potatoes, peeled and thinly sliced

2 white turnips, peeled and thinly sliced

1 garlic clove, minced

1 bay leaf, crumbled

2 tsp sea salt

½ tsp freshly ground pepper

⅓ cup extra-virgin olive oil

1 Tbsp unsalted butter

1 cup equal parts chopped pac choi, salad burnet, and shungiku microgreens

Preheat the oven to 350°F. In a large bowl, combine the potatoes, turnips, garlic, bay leaf, salt, and pepper. Add the oil and toss until the vegetables are coated evenly. Arrange the potatoes and turnips in a shallow baking dish. Add any remaining oil from the bowl and dot with butter. Bake for 20 minutes, add the microgreens, and toss to combine. Continue to bake for 20 to 30 minutes, or until the top is crisp and golden brown. Serve.

Chestnuts and Sprouts

This is a great side dish for fall, when Brussels sprouts are at their sweetest and chestnuts are readily available.

YIELD: 8 SERVINGS

1 lb chestnuts

1¼ lb small Brussels sprouts, trimmed

3 Tbsp (1½ oz) unsalted butter

1 cup equal parts amaranth, cress, mustard, and
    shungiku microgreens

Sea salt and freshly ground pepper

6 bacon slices, fried until crisp

Bring a large saucepan of water to a boil. Using a sharp knife, cut crosses onto the flat sides of the chestnuts. Boil the chestnuts for 15 minutes; drain and remove the skins. Place a steamer basket in the saucepan and add 1 inch of water. Place the chestnuts in the steamer and steam for 10 minutes. Add the Brussels sprouts; continue to steam for 7 to 10 minutes, until the sprouts are tender. Toss the chestnuts and sprouts with the microgreens, butter, and salt and pepper to taste. Crumble the bacon over the vegetables and serve.

Peter Novajosky

sauces

There's not a sauce in creation that would fail to benefit from the addition of a compatible or contrasting microgreen blend to the mix.

Microgreen Pesto

Here's a new twist on an old Italian standby; the celery and Swiss chard micros add a welcome sweetness to the sauce. Serve this over your favorite pasta.

YIELD: 2 CUPS

¼ cup shelled pistachio nuts

¼ cup pine nuts

3 garlic cloves

2 small jalapeño chiles

1 (1-inch) piece fresh ginger, peeled

1¼ cups equal parts basil, celery, and Swiss chard microgreens

3 Tbsp fresh lime juice

1 cup extra-virgin olive oil

Sea salt and freshly ground pepper

Bring a small saucepan of water to a boil, add the pistachios, and cook for 2 minutes. Drain and rub the pistachios briskly between towels to remove their skins. Process the pistachios, pine nuts, garlic, jalapeños, ginger, and microgreens in a food processor or blender until the mixture is a fine paste. Add the lime juice and process for 10 seconds. With the machine running, add the oil in a thin stream until the mixture has a mayonnaise-like consistency. (You may not need the entire cup of oil to obtain the desired result.) Season with salt and pepper to taste.

Microgreen Pesto (left) and
Red Pepper and Mustard
Microgreen Sauce (right)

Henry Beary

Red Pepper and Mustard Microgreen Sauce

This sauce combines the mildly spicy flair of micros and the sweetness of red pepper. It works equally well as a marinade for chicken or fish and as a dressing for salad greens. This recipe calls for a roasted pepper; you can roast, peel, and seed your own or you can buy jarred roasted peppers, which are already peeled.

YIELD: 3 CUPS

2 cups equal parts chopped arugula, beet, and red mustard microgreens

1 roasted red bell pepper (stemmed, peeled, and seeded), cut into thin strips

5 Tbsp light olive oil

5 Tbsp fresh lemon juice

1 garlic clove, finely minced

Sea salt and freshly ground pepper

Process all the ingredients in a blender, mixing until fairly smooth.

(See photograph on page 147)

Mushroom Microgreen Gravy

This is a savory winter gravy to serve over beef, chicken, or veal.

YIELD: 4 CUPS

6 cups chicken stock or broth

1 onion, finely chopped

1 Tbsp extra-virgin olive oil

1 lb shiitake mushrooms, stemmed and finely chopped

⅔ cup dry white wine

1 cup equal parts carrot, celery, and parsley microgreens

Sea salt and freshly ground pepper

In a medium saucepan, bring the broth to a boil. Add the onion and simmer until the liquid is reduced to 3 cups, about 10 minutes. Heat the oil in a large skillet over medium-high heat, add the mushrooms, and cook, stirring, for 10 minutes. Add the broth with onion, the wine, and the microgreens. Simmer for 10 more minutes and season with salt and pepper to taste.

Henry Beary

dressings

Like sauces, salad dressings gain surprising piquancy and depth when prepared with freshly harvested micros.

Microgreen Fines Herbes Dressing

Here's a good all-purpose white wine dressing with countless applications. It's especially good over grilled chicken, fish, or vegetables, as well as on salads.

YIELD: 2 CUPS

½ cup dry white wine

2 Tbsp fresh lemon juice

2 Tbsp (1 oz) unsalted butter

2 shallots, minced

1 small tomato, peeled, seeded, and coarsely chopped

1 garlic clove, minced

¼ cup crème fraîche or sour cream

1 cup equal parts chopped chervil, garlic chive, parsley, and Mexican tarragon microgreens

In a small saucepan, combine the wine, lemon juice, butter, shallots, tomato, and garlic. Bring to a boil; then reduce the heat and simmer uncovered for 20 minutes. Strain the sauce through a fine sieve into a bowl. Whisk in the crème fraîche and stir in the microgreens. Return the dressing to the saucepan and heat over low heat just until warmed through; do not boil.

Henry Beary

Classic Balsamic Dressing with Micros

This is another versatile salad dressing, good for special occasions and for everyday meals.

YIELD: 1 CUP

¼ cup sour cream

1 Tbsp balsamic vinegar

1 Tbsp extra-virgin olive oil

1 shallot, peeled

1 garlic clove, peeled

1 tsp Dijon mustard

1 cup equal parts chopped sorrel, lemon basil, and parsley microgreens

Sea salt and freshly ground pepper

Process the sour cream, vinegar, oil, shallot, garlic, and mustard in a blender or food processor until smooth. Add the microgreens and season with salt and pepper to taste. Refrigerate until ready to serve.

Walnut Oil and Raspberry Vinegar Dressing

Everyone has a favorite go-to salad dressing and this one is mine, mainly because I love the flavor of walnut oil, which should be enjoyed at room temperature or slightly warmed. A worthy alternative to lemon juice or olive oil, this dressing is a great way to take advantage of a surplus of any favorite blend of salad greens or microgreens. Any extra dressing can be stored in the refrigerator for up to two weeks.

YIELD 1 CUP

1 cup walnut oil
2 Tbsp raspberry vinegar
Sea salt and freshly ground pepper

Whisk the oil and vinegar together in a medium bowl and season with salt and pepper to taste.

Adams Road Salad Dressing

This tangy all-purpose dressing is named for our farm's location in Easton, Connecticut.

YIELD: 1 CUP

¾ cup extra-virgin olive oil

2 Tbsp white wine vinegar

¼ cup parsley microgreens

¼ cup scallion microgreens

¼ cup garlic chive microgreens

1 tsp sea salt

¼ tsp freshly ground pepper

2 Tbsp sour cream or plain yogurt

Process the oil, microgreens, vinegar, salt, and pepper in a blender or food processor for 5 to 10 seconds. With the machine running, add the sour cream and process another 5 seconds. Pour into an airtight jar and refrigerate for at least 2 hours before serving.

sandwiches

Substitute your own micros for store-bought greens to give instant crunch and unexpected flavor to your favorite sandwiches.

Grilled Eggplant and Cheese Sandwich with Asian Micros

Here's a sandwich you'll want to roll your sleeves up and make for special occasions. Eggplant has been cultivated in India for thousands of years. Blessed with an intriguing flavor and rich in anti-oxidants, it offers many culinary opportunities and blends well with a wide range of microgreens. If you're able to find it, I recommend using Duke's Mayonnaise, a flavorful spread popular in the South. Also, this recipe calls for roasted garlic, which you may want to prepare ahead of time. To roast a head of garlic, place it in a 350-degree oven for 1 hour. Let the garlic cool; separate the cloves, and squeeze them from their papery skins before mashing them.

YIELD: 4 SERVINGS

1 lb Asian eggplants, cut horizontally into ¼-inch-thick slices

Extra-virgin olive oil or nonstick olive oil spray

1 head garlic, roasted, cloves removed from skins and mashed

2 Tbsp mayonnaise

1 tsp balsamic or sherry vinegar

1 whole-wheat baguette, about 18 inches long

2 oz fresh goat cheese, homemade yogurt cheese, or feta cheese, crumbled

¼ cup pac choi microgreens

¼ cup shungiku microgreens

Preheat a grill to medium heat or preheat the broiler. Spray or lightly brush both sides of the eggplant slices with the oil. Cook the eggplant 3 to 5 minutes, or until tender and golden, turning once. Transfer the eggplant to a platter. In a small bowl, whisk together the roasted garlic, mayonnaise, and vinegar.

Cut the baguette into 4 pieces and halve each piece horizontally. Spread the bottom halves with the mayonnaise mixture. Add the eggplant slices, trimming to fit if necessary, and sprinkle each sandwich with crumbled cheese and microgreens. Cover with the remaining bread slices. Cut each sandwich in half and serve.

Rebecca's Roast Beef Special

One of my nine granddaughters, Rebecca, came up with this sandwich one day after her mother, Celeste, came home from our farm with a bag of mixed microgreens. You can choose the amounts of oil, beef, and cheese and the variety of microgreens to suit your tastes and appetite.

YIELD: 1 SERVING

2 slices crusty Italian or Portuguese bread

Extra-virgin olive oil infused with herbs

Sliced roast beef

Sharp cheddar cheese, thinly sliced

⅓ cup microgreens

Toast the bread and brush with oil. Add slices of roast beef and cheddar to 1 slice of bread and top with the microgreens. Top with the second slice of bread and serve.

Henry Beary

Henry Beary

Fried Green Tomato and Basil Sandwich

A Southern staple with the kick of microgreens. If you're able to find it, I recommend using Duke's Mayonnaise, a flavorful spread popular in the South.

YIELD: 4 SERVINGS

1 cup unbleached all-purpose flour

1 tsp sea salt

⅛ tsp freshly ground pepper

⅔ cup buttermilk

Canola oil

4 green tomatoes (about 2 lb), cored and sliced ½ inch thick

8 slices whole-wheat bread

2 Tbsp mayonnaise

1½ cups basil and mustard microgreens, or enough to dress 4 sandwiches

Combine the flour, salt, and pepper in a shallow bowl. Pour the buttermilk into a second shallow bowl. Pour enough oil into a large, heavy skillet to reach a depth of ⅛ inch and heat over high heat until a speck of flour dropped in the oil "dances."

Dip the tomato slices in the buttermilk, then in the flour mixture, coating both sides. Carefully add the tomato slices to the skillet and lower the heat to medium. Fry the tomatoes until golden brown on one side, then turn and fry until golden on the other side. Remove with a slotted spatula and drain on paper towels.

Lightly toast the bread. Spread the mayonnaise on 4 slices of the toast and top each with a handful of microgreens. Add the tomato slices and top with the remaining slices of toast. Cut the sandwiches in half and serve.

Henry Beary

smoothies

Smoothies are a fun way to pack the nutrients of microgreens into delicious beverage form. Some people swear by them for breakfast, but they can be enjoyed at any time of day.

Smoothies can be mixed using the blenders found in most kitchens these days. More powerful (and more expensive) juicers are necessary to break down microgreens such as wheatgrass and other hard or fibrous vegetables. Fruit like banana, papaya, mango, and peach add a creamy texture to smoothies. So does avocado. Other fruits, such as pear, apple, pineapple, and blueberry, all may be used to add color and flavor to smoothies.

Using frozen fruit has the advantage of chilling your smoothie. If fresh fruit is used, add ice cubes to give the drink a refreshing chill.

To boost nutritional content, blend microgreens, leafy greens like baby spinach, or any other green vegetable in with the mix. A 3:1 to 3:2 ratio of fruits to vegetables will provide you with a drink that tastes good and is really good for you, too.

Coconut water and milk derived from nuts, such as almonds or hazelnuts, are good substitutes for dairy products in blender recipes.

Mint and Melon Shake

YIELD: 1 SERVING

¼ cup mint leaves

¼ cup sorrel microgreens, or 1 Tbsp lovage
   microgreens

1 cup honeydew melon chunks

½ cup plain or vanilla yogurt

1 tsp minced fresh ginger

1 tsp honey

5 or 6 ice cubes

Place all the ingredients in a blender and process
until smooth. Serve.

Henry Beary

Mango Tango

YIELD: 1 SERVING

1 cup frozen mango chunks

½ banana

½ cup amaranth, red-veined sorrel, and purple basil microgreens

1–2 cups milk or coconut water

Juice of ½ lemon

Place all the ingredients in a blender and process until smooth. Serve.

Wake Up and Smell the Micros Cocktail

YIELD: 1 SERVING

1 cup equal parts kale, mustard, and nasturtium
    microgreens
2 celery stalks, chopped
1 tart apple, peeled, seeded and chopped
Juice of 1 lime
Freshly ground white pepper
Chili powder or paprika, for sprinkling (optional)

Place all the ingredients in a blender and process
until smooth. Sprinkle chili powder or paprika on
top, if desired, and serve. Gesundheit!

Henry Beary

Acknowledgments

The authors had a lot of help putting this book together. In particular, we send our sincere thanks and appreciation to the following people:

Henry G. Beary and Peter Novajosky, for the many photos that enliven these pages.

Dawn Totora and Coleen O'Shea, for their creative styling of the recipe photographs.

Sal's son, Sal, for his expert work on the grill, and grandson, Bilal, for all his culinary skills.

Kathryn Precourt, for reviewing our microgreen recipes and for lending table settings and other decorations to make the recipes look even more delectable.

Everyone at Gilbertie's who helped get our microgreens business going and who helped to make this book happen. Thank you, Jan, Carol, Stephen, Dan, Louie, Emily, John, Arlene, Eddie, Berta, Sarah, Brandon, Martha, Yolanda, Augie, and Baudie, plus our amazing office staff of Marie, Lynn, and Jeanne. Special thanks to Renee Giroux, who convinced Sal to grow microgreens for cutting when he wasn't sure there was much of a market for them.

Thanks also for all the support we received from The Countryman Press, including Lisa Sacks, Melissa Dobson, Cheryl Redmond, Vicky Shea, and especially Kermit Hummel, who believed in our book from the first and even made the trek to the Gilbertie farm in Connecticut to see for himself our microgreens in all their glory.

Last, but not least, we again thank Coleen O'Shea, in her capacity as our agent, for her patience and perspicacity in guiding us through this project from beginning to end.

Index

Note: Page references in *italics* refer to photographs of recipes.